100 GREATS
WORCESTERSHIRE
COUNTY CRICKET CLUB

The County Champions in 1964. From left to right, back row: Norman Gifford, Ron Headley, Alan Ormrod, Bob Carter, Len Coldwell, Jim Standen, Dick Richardson, Doug Slade. Front row: Roy Booth, Tom Graveney, Don Kenyon (captain), Jack Flavell, Martin Horton.

New Road reunion, twenty years later. From left to right, back row: Duncan Fearnley, Brian Brain, Bob Carter, Basil D'Oliveira, Doug Slade, Joe Lister, John Elliott. Front row: Martin Horton, Jack Flavell, Tom Graveney, Don Kenyon, Roy Booth, Len Coldwell, Dick Richardson.

100 GREATS

WORCESTERSHIRE
COUNTY CRICKET CLUB

LES HATTON

For Bernard,
Thank you for your help
with the 'top twenty' and
for the photographs.
Best wishes
Les Hatton

TEMPUS

Tempus Publishing Limited
The Mill, Brimscombe Port,
Stroud, Gloucestershire, GL5 2QG

ISBN 0 7524 2194 8

Typesetting and origination by
Tempus Publishing Limited
Printed in Great Britain by
Midway Colour Print, Wiltshire

Present and forthcoming cricket titles from Tempus Publishing:

0 7524 2166 2	A False Stroke of Genius: The Wayne Larkins Story	John Wallace	£12.99
0 7524 1639	The Australians in England	William Powell	£9.99
0 7524 0792 9	Glamorgan County Cricket Club	Andrew Hignell	£9.99
0 7524 1137 3	Glamorgan County Cricket Club II	Andrew Hignell	£9.99
0 7524 1879 3	Glamorgan CCC: 100 Greats	Andrew Hignell	£9.99
0 7524 2182 4	Glamorgan CCC: Classics	Andrew Hignell	£12.00
0 7524 1876 9	Hampshire County Cricket Club	N. Jenkinson, D. Allen & A. Renishaw	£9.99
0 7524 2188 3	Hampshire CCC: 100 Greats	N. Jenkinson, D. Allen & A. Renishaw	£12.00
0 7524 2167 0	Lord's: Cathedral of Cricket (hb)	Stephen Green	£25.00
0 7524 1871 8	Kent County Cricket Club	William Powell	£9.99
0 7524 1864 5	Leicestershire County Cricket Club	Dennis Lambert	£9.99
0 7524 2175 1	Leicestershire CCC: 100 Greats	Dennis Lambert	£12.00
0 7524 2195 6	Northamptonshire CCC: 100 Greats	Andrew Radd	£12.00
0 7524 1638 3	The Scarborough Cricket Festival	William Powell	£9.99
0 7524 1585 9	Somerset County Cricket Club	Somerset Cricket Museum	£9.99
0 7524 2178 6	Somerset CCC: 100 Greats	Eddie Lawrence	£12.00
0 7524 2192 1	Sussex County Cricket Club	John Wallace	£10.99
0 7524 1885 8	Varsity Cricket	William Powell	£9.99
0 7524 2180 8	Warwickshire CCC: 100 Greats	Robert Brooke	£12.00
0 7524 1834 3	Worcestershire County Cricket Club	Les Hatton	£9.99
0 7524 0756 2	Yorkshire County Cricket Club	Mick Pope	£9.99
0 7524 2179 4	Yorkshire CCC: 100 Greats	Mick Pope & Paul Dyson	£12.00

PREFACE

This book outlines the deeds of 100 out of the 462 cricketers who have represented Worcestershire in first-class cricket since the visit of Yorkshire to New Road in May 1899. The Foster brothers from Malvern were prominent in the early years and four of them feature in this selection. The seasons following the First World War were very humble days for the club, with places in the lower reaches of the Championship table a regular occurrence. Fred Root carried the responsibility of the bowling during this period until Reg Perks arrived in 1930, with 'Doc' Gibbons and Cyril Walters scoring most of the runs up to the beginning of the Second World War. Immediately after the war Don Kenyon came on the scene and when he took over the captaincy in 1959, a Championship-winning side was beginning to develop. Back to back titles were won in 1964 and 1965, sandwiched in between two Lord's Gillette Cup final defeats in 1963 and 1966. Norman Gifford was an integral part of that side and later in 1974 he led them to the third of their Championship titles after they had enjoyed one-day success in the John Player League in 1971, helped by some great starts by Glenn Turner and his opening partner Ron Headley. The next successful captain was Phil Neale, who led them to the Sunday League title in 1987, the Championship and League double in 1988 and another Championship in 1989. At Lord's in 1991 the run of six defeats ended with a 65 runs win over Lancashire in the Benson & HedgesTrophy with Phil taking the catch to dismiss Paul Allott, the last Lancashire wicket, off Graham Dilley. Tim Curtis and Graeme Hick were now scoring the runs and Neal Radford and Phil Newport were ably supported by Richard Illingworth with the ball. Fresh in everyone's mind is Glen McGrath's performance in 2000 with 80 first-class wickets at an average of 13.21 and 34 one-day wickets at an average of 9.14. I might well be criticised for leaving McGrath out of the top twenty, but I found that the most difficult part of this book was the selection of these chosen few. After much deliberation, I decided that the best way out of the dilemma would be to form a panel of six dedicated watchers of Worcestershire cricket, hear their twenty choices, and go from there. All of us, Bernard Bridgewater, Bob Brookes, Don Cairney, Jack Godfrey, Paul Lockley and myself, chose Ted Arnold, Basil D'Oliveira, Jack Flavell, Tom Graveney, Graeme Hick, Dick Howorth, Don Kenyon, Reg Perks and Fred Root and five of us went for 'Doc' Gibbons, 'Roly' Jenkins and Glenn Turner but altogether thirty-five different names were suggested by the six of us.

ACKNOWLEDGEMENTS AND BIBLIOGRAPHY

My thanks go first of all to Tim Curtis for writing the foreword and to James Howarth of Tempus for his encouragement in the production of this book. Many of the photographs are out of the archives at New Road, and for them I give most grateful thanks to Michael Vockins and Joan Grundy. Thanks also to Jean Kenyon, Bernard Bridgewater and Jack Godfrey for the use of photographs from their collections and to Roy Booth, Robert Brooke and Martin Horton for their help during several telephone conversations.

For other photographs I would like to help Tom Bader, *Berrows Journal*, *Worcester Evening News*, *The Black Country Bugle*, Central Press, Patrick Eagar, Les Jaques, Ken Kelly, Roger Wootton, Susanne Marlow, Sport and General, Universal Press and Albert Wilkes. Facts and figures were derived from various sources, including:

Images of Sport, Worcestershire County Cricket Club by Les Hatton (Tempus 1999)
Worcestershire County Cricket Club by David Lemmon (Christopher Helm 1989)
Worcestershire County Cricket Club, First-Class Records by Les Hatton (Limlow Books 1996)
Who's Who of Cricketers by Philip Bailey, Philip Thorn and Peter Wynne-Thomas (Hamlyn 1993)
The Wisden Book of Test Cricket,1877-1977 by Bill Frindall (Macdonald and Janes 1979)
Wisden's Cricketers' Almanac (various years)
Worcestershire County Cricket Club Yearbooks 1928-2000
Three Black Pears, Worcestershire CCC 1998 by Bernard Bridgewater

Statistical Note:
All the career statistics are correct to 1 October 2000, and refer to performances for Worcestershire CCC in first class cricket since 1899, the Sunday/National League, the Benson & Hedges Cup, the Gillette Cup and the NatWest Trophy.

Key
The letters at the top of the page refer to the following batting or bowling styles:

RHB – right-handed batsman
LHB – left-handed batsman
OB – off-break bowler
SLA – slow left arm spin
RFM – right-arm fast medium
RF – right-arm fast
LF – left-arm fast
LM – left-arm medium pace
RM – right-arm medium pace
LB – leg break bowler
WK – wicketkeeper
* – not out

FOREWORD BY TIM CURTIS

To be asked to write a foreword for a book celebrating the great players of my county and by someone who has been such a quietly devoted and knowledgeable follower of that county as Les Hatton is both a great delight and a privilege.

My first visit to New Road was to watch the last appearance of Tom Graveney. The fact that my father, a Bristolian, took me, hints at Tom's dual county career. He was not the first, nor the last in a line of adopted sons who have graced Worcestershire's colours and blossomed in the benevolent atmosphere of the New Road ground. In 1979, when I started, I saw Basil D'Oliveira finishing against Sri Lanka with a hundred, scored with all his customary flamboyant power, apparently undimmed by the years. He was a wonderful entertainer, delighting as much with his athleticism in the outfield as with the belligerence of his batting.

Glenn Turner flayed county attacks in my early years. From stonewall defence he emerged as one of the finest attacking batsmen of his generation, with a trademark square drive played off one knee and an early delight in improvising one-day shots. Typically innovative, these he shaped out of a batting style which was very much his own, the success of which was marked by his certain progress towards that special band of players who have scored 100 centuries.

And then there was Graeme Hick, joining Turner as the scorer of 100 centuries at a younger age than all but Hammond, and in fewer innings than all but Bradman and Compton. I had occasion to see him more than most and he never ceased to amaze me with his unerring eye, timing and the searing power of his stroke play. He, more than any other individual, was responsible for Worcestershire's success in the golden period of the late 1980s.

Yet Worcestershire has produced many of its own of whom it can be justifiably proud. Jack Flavell, strong, skilful and aggressive, led an attack which took Worcestershire to back to back championships in the 1960s and his captain was Don Kenyon. In later years, as president of the club, I savoured the proud and steely glint in Don Kenyon's eyes as he scored every run again, whilst watching those who sought to match his deeds and elegant stroke play for the county which he loved. And I was proud to be a listener when Roly Jenkins spun the ball lovingly in his gnarled but still strong fingers and tried to impart some of his fantastic passion for the game and the art of leg spin bowling.

They were masters all of their trade, great players for Worcestershire and internationals in their own right. There are many others I would love to have known or played with, but I write of those whom I feel qualified to say something about. I am privileged to be in their company. I could never approach Tom Graveney's style, although I hope that I might one day blossom as I saw Glenn Turner do. Perhaps my writing developed more than my batting! Worcestershire is a wonderful county with a proud history and this book stands as a fitting tribute to the players who have shaped that history.

100 WORCESTERSHIRE GREATS

Hartley Alleyne
Ted Arnold
Ernie Bale
Paul Bent
Roy Berry
Albert Bird
Ronnie Bird
Roy Booth
Ian Botham
Fred Bowley
Brian Brain
Bob Broadbent
George Brook
Charlie Bull
Syd Buller
William Burns
Dick Burrows
Bob Carter
Frank Chester
Len Coldwell
Eddie Cooper
Jack Cuffe
Jim Cumbes
Tim Curtis
George Dews
Graham Dilley
Basil D'Oliveira
Damian D'Oliveira
Duncan Fearnley
Jack Flavell
Geoff Foster
Harry Foster
Maurice Foster
Tip Foster

Vic Fox
George Gaukrodger
Doc Gibbons
Norman Gifford
Tom Graveney
Ron Headley
Ted Hemsley
Graeme Hick
Bunny Higgins
Vanburn Holder
Martin Horton
Dick Howorth
David Humphries
Fred Hunt
Richard Illingworth
Imran Khan
John Inchmore
Peter Jackson
Roly Jenkins
Maurice Jewell
Kapil Dev
Don Kenyon
Stuart Lampitt
David Leatherdale
Joe Lister
Gordon Lord
Charles Lyttelton
Glen McGrath
Sid Martin
Tom Moody
Phil Neale
Phil Newport
Maurice Nichol
Alan Ormrod

Laddie Outschoorn
Charlie Palmer
Nawab of Pataudi
Dipak Patel
Dick Pearson
Reg Perks
Cecil Ponsonby
Charles Preece
Paul Pridgeon
Bernard Quaife
Neal Radford
Steve Rhodes
Dick Richardson
Peter Richardson
Fred Root
George Simpson-Hayward
Doug Slade
David Smith
Vikram Solanki
Jim Standen
Tom Straw
Percy Tarbox
Glenn Turner
Cyril Walters
Martin Weston
Fred Wheldon
Norman Whiting
Gordon Wilcock
George Wilson
Bob Wyatt
Hugo Yarnold
Younis Ahmed

The top 20, who appear here in italics, are all afforded extra coverage.

Hartley Alleyne
RHB & RFM, 1980-82

Born: Barbados, 28 February 1957						
Batting career:						
M	**I**	**NO**	**Runs**	**Av**	**50**	
38	41	8	398	12.06	1	
39	*24*	*5*	*198*	*10.42*	*-*	
100	**Ct/St**					
-	7					
-	*5*					
Bowling career:						
O	**M**	**R**	**W**	**Av**	**5wl**	**10wM**
1053.1	207	3222	119	27.07	5	2
316.1	*34*	*1130*	*46*	*24.56*	*-*	*-*

Career best performances:

72 v. Lancashire, Stourport-on-Severn 1980

8-43 v. Middlesex, Lord's 1981

32 v. Kent, Worcester 1980

4-24 v. Lancashire, Worcester 1980

Hartley Alleyne made his debut for Worcestershire at New Road against Gloucestershire, with Sadiq Mohammed the first of his 64 wickets that season. He proved a fine overseas replacement for Vanburn Holder. The last two wickets of his career best figures of 8 for 43 at Lord's in July 1981 were John Emburey and Bill Merry with consecutive balls to finish off the Middlesex first innings. With the first ball of their second innings he bowled Graham Barlow to complete the hat-trick. He followed this with the wicket of Clive Radley before he had scored, but during his fourth over he fell heavily and had to leave the field. He didn't bowl again during that innings and he made only occasional appearances afterwards.

When Worcestershire made their one and only visit to the Chain Wire Ground at Stourport-on-Severn in 1980, Lancashire were the visitors and Alleyne shared a seventh wicket partnership of 146 in 96 minutes with David Humphries. It is still the best for this wicket by Worcestershire against Lancashire, with Humphries scoring 108 not out and Alleyne a career best 72, hitting 5 sixes and 6 fours. Heavy rain over the weekend prevented play on the Monday, and Norman Gifford with 10 for 40 in the match bowled the visitors to an innings defeat after Alleyne had begun their second innings downfall, taking the wickets of David Lloyd and Andrew Kennedy.

Always an enthusiastic cricketer, Alleyne had only three seasons with Worcestershire before he was released, having taken just 16 wickets in 1982. Before he joining Worcestershire he had played for Lincolnshire in 1979, having made his first-class debut for Barbados against the Combined Islands in 1978/79 and going on tour to Zimbabwe with Young West Indies in 1981/82. Following his departure from New Road, he went on the second West Indies tour of South Africa in 1983/84 under the leadership of Lawrence Rowe and played in the last two 'Tests', with a best performance of 5 for 62 at The Wanderers. The following winter saw him return to South Africa to join Natal, for whom he played until the end of the 1989/90 season, having a career best score of 5 for 103 against Western Province during his first season with them. During this period in South Africa he appeared for Buckinghamshire between 1984 and 1986 and joined Kent for the summers of 1988 and 1989. His first-class career ended with his departure from Natal, having taken a total of 254 wickets at an average of 27.66.

Ted Arnold

RHB & RFM, 1899-1913

Born: Exmouth, Devon, 7 November 1876
Died: Worcester, 25 October 1942

Batting career:

M	I	NO	Runs	Av	50
301	527	54	14825	31.34	70
100	**Ct/St**				
24	158				

Bowling career:

O	M	R	W	Av	5wl	10wM
8057.4	2007	21401	902	23.72	56	12

Career best performances:

215 v. Oxford University, Oxford,1910
9-64 v. Oxford University, Oxford,1905

After a spell with Devon, Ted Arnold joined Worcestershire and made his debut for them during their Minor Counties days in June 1895 at Christchurch College, Oxford against Oxfordshire. He opened the innings, scoring 17 and 20, and taking 2-2 in the home side's first innings. Two years later he became the only Worcestershire bowler at any level to take all ten wickets in an innings when he had figures of 10 for 54 at Northampton. Following their triumph in the Minor Counties Championship in 1896, 1897 and 1898, Worcestershire were elevated to the County Championship and Arnold appeared in their first match, at New Road in May 1899 against Yorkshire. His first first-class wicket was that of Wilfred Rhodes and at the end of the season he had scored 794 runs and taken 48 wickets, scoring two centuries and having a five-in-a-single-innings performance.

In 1903 he became the first Worcestershire cricketer to complete the 1,000 runs/100 wickets double, having been just three wickets short of it the previous season. His final aggregates were 1,040 runs and 125 wickets, the highlights being a hundred in each innings against Cambridge University, Arnold being the first to achieve this at Fenner's; and 12 for 79 in the match against Warwickshire, which helped Worcestershire to their first win at Edgbaston. This was his only double for Worcestershire, although he had completed one in 1902 and did so again in 1904 and 1905. At Lord's and at The Oval in 1903 Arnold played for the Players against the Gentlemen and also for the Rest against the Champions at Middlesex.

His exploits in 1903 were rewarded with an MCC tour to Australia in the winter of 1903/04 with colleague 'Tip' Foster also on board. They both shone on their Test debuts at Sydney, with a double-century by Foster; Arnold had the prize wicket of Victor Trumper with his first ball in Test cricket, caught by Foster. Arnold scored 27 in his only innings, and took 4 for 76 and 2 for 93. He finished with 18 wickets at an average of 26.38 from four Tests and England won the series 3-2. In between the Third and Fourth Tests, the MCC played Victoria at Melbourne and Arnold and Wilfred Rhodes caused havoc. Victoria were dismissed for 15 in their second innings, which is still the lowest total in Australian first-class cricket, with Rhodes taking 5 for 6 off 6.1 overs and Arnold 4 for 8 off 6. He played in six more Test matches after his return home, all in England, four more against Australia and two against South Africa.

Arnold had his career best performance at Oxford in May 1905, in the second of the

University's innings when they were chasing 377 to win. He bowled unchanged for his 9-64 and Worcestershire won by 211 runs. John Cuffe helped Arnold to a unique Worcestershire bowling performance at Park Avenue, Bradford when they bowled throughout the match against Yorkshire in August 1907. In the first innings Arnold had 6 for 22 and Cuffe 4 for 38 and in the second Arnold had 1 for 44 and Cuffe 9 for 38 to set up a 30 runs win. They completed their first double over Yorkshire having won on the opening day of the season at New Road by 54 runs, where Arnold had figures of 5 for 59 and 3 for 68.

Arnold's all-round ability was emphatically illustrated when Worcestershire went to Edgbaston in August 1909. Warwickshire batted first and were dismissed for 141, Arnold taking 3 for 70. Worcestershire had lost their first four wickets for 83 runs when William Burns joined Arnold for what was to be a English record partnership for eighty-nine years, until it was beaten by Mal Loye and David Ripley with 401 for Northamptonshire against Glamorgan in 1998. They added 393 for the fifth wicket in four and three quarter hours, with Arnold striking a five and 14 fours in an unbeaten 200. Burns was eventually bowled by Charles Baker for 196 and the visitors declared at 578 for 6, with a lead of 437 runs. Arnold then destroyed Warwickshire with 7 for 44 in their second innings and the game was over shortly after lunch on the third day. This fine all-rounder became the first Worcestershire cricketer to score more than one hundred runs and take ten wickets in the same match, an achievement that remained a one-off until Imran Khan's performance against Lancashire in 1976.

The following season after this maiden double-century saw Arnold reach a career best 215 at Oxford, with the University once again suffering at his expense. He opened with 'Dick' Pearson, adding 161 for the first wicket, Geoffrey Foster went before he had even scored and Arnold then was joined by Burns. This did not quite match the epic stand of 1909, although a useful 105 was added for the third wicket with Burns. Arnold had hit 2 sixes and 29 fours when he was seventh out at 350,

having been dropped at 28 and 48.

He scored 1,000 runs in a season seven times for Worcestershire and took 100 wickets twice, but he had below par seasons in 1912 and 1913 and was released at the end of the latter. In his first-class career he scored 15,853 runs at an average of 29.91, took 1,069 wickets at an average of 23.16 and held 187 catches. He remained in Worcester after leaving the game and he died on 25 October 1942 at the age of sixty-five, having long suffered from poor health. Two of his nephews, John Price (1927-29) and William Price (1923) played for Worcestershire.

Ernest Bale
RHB & WK, 1908-20

Born: Mitcham, Surrey, 18 September 1878
Died: Carshalton, Surrey, 6 July 1952

Batting career:

M	I	NO	Runs	Av	50
138	217	79	1096	7.95	-

100	Ct/St
-	234/85

Bowling career:

O	M	R	W	Av	5wl	10wM
53	3	217	8	27.12	-	-

Career best performances:

43 v. South Africans, Worcester, 1912
3-46 v. H.K. Foster's XI, Hereford, 1919

Ernest Bale left his home county after just one match against Oxford University at The Oval in 1904, feeling that it was highly unlikely that he would ever be called upon to replace Herbert Strudwick, the regular Surrey, and future England, wicketkeeper. That season he had six games for London County with 11 catches and 4 stumpings and a best score with the bat of 22* against Leicestershire.

Joining Worcestershire in 1908 and making his debut at Lord's against the MCC, he shared wicketkeeping duties with George Gaukrodger until he took over in 1910, when he became a fixture in the side. Always a lower order batsman and never finishing a season with an average in double figures, he had his career-best batting against the touring South Africans at New Road in 1912. In the first innings Sid Pegler had destroyed the Worcestershire batting with 7 for 31, Bale 1* in an all out total of 50 and following an opening partnership of 126 by Herbie Taylor (83) and Gerald Hartigan (103), Worcestershire began their second innings 248 runs behind. When Bale joined Dick Burrows, 88 runs were required to make the tourists bat again and, despite a ninth wicket partnership of 77 in 45 minutes, Worcestershire lost by an innings and 42 runs. Burrows hit 45 and Bale 43 before being bowled by Pegler, his second wicket giving him match figures of 9 for 75.

During the 1911 season he took 57 dismissals, 40 caught and 17 stumped, to create a Worcestershire record, one more than Tom Straw had collected in 1901. At the end of the 1913 season he had done even better, with 48 catches and 9 stumpings, which was a Worcestershire record that remained until it was beaten by Syd Buller with 62 – 44 catches and 18 stumpings – in 1937.

After the First World War he took part in Worcestershire's short season of two-day friendlies. In the match at Hereford he came on to bowl in the second innings of the match against an eleven raised by H.K. Foster. Worcestershire were on their way to a four-wicket defeat when Bale had career best figures of 3 for 46. One more season followed when he made three appearances but only one with the gloves. He had been replaced by Arthur Jewell, brother of Maurice, who began with a century on his County Championship debut, 110 at New Road against Hampshire, the only Worcestershire batsman to do this.

On leaving the game, he entered the family furniture business in Surrey and died in July 1952 at the age of seventy-three.

Paul Bent
RHB & OB, 1985-91

Born: Worcester, 1 May 1965

Batting career:

M	I	NO	Runs	Av	50
32	54	2	1289	24.78	6
3	*3*	*0*	*51*	*17.00*	*-*

100	Ct/St
2	4
-	*3*

Bowling career:

O	M	R	W	5wl	10wM
3	1	5	0	-	-

Career best performances:

144 v. Kent, Worcester, 1989

36 v. Sussex, Worcester, 1988

In 1985, Paul Bent made his first-class debut for Worcestershire at Fenner's in a match that has some question about its status. The First XI opted to play two meaningless one-day games at New Road against the touring Zimbabweans on the same dates as the first two days of the University fixture. This meant that an inexperienced side went to Cambridge to fulfil the fixture, which gave seven youngsters their first-class debut, three of whom never played in another. Rain, however, ruined the game and in the one Worcestershire innings Bent scored 14 out of a total of 216 for 5 declared. There then followed a couple of seasons on the MCC ground staff with the Young Professionals and he didn't make his Championship debut until July 1988, when he scored 31 and 50 in a 21 runs win over Yorkshire at New Road. There followed two more games and a share of the celebrations when the county beat Glamorgan for their first County Championship title since 1974.

His best season was 1989, when they won the County Championship once again and he hit his maiden century against Kent at New Road. He came into the side in place of Tim Curtis who was playing against the Australians in the Old Trafford Test, and shared an opening partnership of 113 with Chris Tolley and one of 135 for the second with Graeme Hick. His 144 came off 202 balls and included 22 fours; Kent were forced to follow-on and were eventually beaten by ten wickets.

Earlier that season, history was made as three former Worcester Royal Grammar School boys played in the same Worcestershire First XI when Bent, Tim Curtis and Steve McEwan all appeared against Middlesex at New Road. In 1934 Old Elizabethans Cyril Harrison and Montague White appeared together in three matches at Cheltenham, Bradford and at Worcester against Kent.

At Blackpool in 1991 Bent shared an opening partnership of 225 with Curtis, a stand equalling Worcestershire's best against Lancashire previously shared by Cyril Walters and 'Doc' Gibbons at Worcester in 1933. Curtis scored 120 and declared shortly after when Bent reached a century. The match was drawn, however, when rain took the players off, with Lancashire requiring 11 to win off three overs with three wickets remaining.

Bent left at the end of the 1991 season and played six matches for Herefordshire in 1992, their first season in the Minor Counties Championship. He is now a policeman stationed at Kidderminster.

Roy Berry
LHB & SLA, 1955-58

Born: Manchester, 29 January 1926

Batting career:

M	I	NO	Runs	Av	50
94	118	40	601	7.70	-

100	Ct/St
-	34

Bowling career:

O	M	R	W	Av	5wI	10wM
2948.1	1150	6263	250	25.05	13	2

Career best performances:

32 v. Somerset, Worcester, 1957
6-37 v. Gloucestershire, Bristol, 1956

Roy Berry joined Worcestershire after a successful career with Lancashire between 1948 and 1954, for whom he took 259 wickets at 22.77. At Blackpool in 1953 he took all ten Worcestershire second innings wickets for 102 and when he made his debut for Worcestershire against the South Africans in 1955, seven of them were his colleagues. He took 5 for 60 in the first inning and 1 for 27 in the second innings, helping his new club to a 117 runs victory, the only county side to beat the tourists during that season.

His best performance for Worcestershire was recorded the following season, when he took 6 for 37 against Gloucestershire at Bristol in the second innings, having taken 5 for 64 in the first – sadly, his efforts were in vain. Worcestershire lost by 131 runs when they were dismissed for 64 in their first innings, with John Mortimore taking 6 for 30, and for 95 in the second, when Sam Cook took 7 for 27 (10 for 35 in the match).

At Kidderminster in 1957, Berry improved on those Bristol match figures with 11 for 142 against Middlesex, including Denis Compton, caught and bowled in the first innings and stumped by Roy Booth in the second. Compton scored 48 in the first innings and 82 in the second. His whirlwind 48 came off just thirteen scoring shots, with 3 sixes and 5 fours off Berry. Figures of 5 for 66 in the first innings and 6 for 76 in the second were sadly not supported by the batsmen, and the visitors won comfortably by 134 runs. He finished the season with his best haul with 87 wickets, 76 of them in the Championship. During that season he had his best Worcestershire performance with the bat when he hit 32 and helped Roly Jenkins add 90 for the eighth wicket against Somerset at New Road, but Worcestershire were beaten once again. In fact, of the 13 five-wicket performances by Berry for Worcestershire, only twice was he on the winning side – his debut match against the South Africans and at Kidderminster against Yorkshire in 1956. In this match he took 5 for 45 in the first innings, after Don Kenyon had slaughtered the Yorkshire bowling with an innings of 259, and Martin Horton took 5 for 64 in the second to inflict an innings defeat on the White Rose county.

Berry left Worcestershire at the end of the 1958, having taken only 25 wickets, and he then spent four seasons with Derbyshire before retiring to manage the Rushey Hotel in Mansfield.

Albert Bird

RHB & OB, 1899-1909

Born: Moseley, Birmingham, 17 August 1867
Died: Worcester, 17 June 1927

Batting career:

M	I	NO	Runs	Av	50
143	225	63	1951	12.04	2

100	Ct/St
-	55

Bowling career:

O	M	R	W	Av	5wl	10wM
2657.5	576	7403	292	25.35	20	3

Career best performances:

64* v. Lancashire, Worcester, 1902
7-41 v. Oxford University, Oxford, 1903

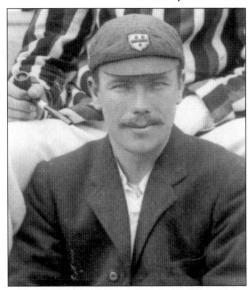

Albert Bird was a member of the Worcestershire side that met Yorkshire at New Road in May 1899, the first first-class fixture played by the county. By then he was over thirty, having played for Warwickshire in non-first-class matches between 1887 and 1890 and for Worcestershire similarly from 1894, when he first appeared for Paul Foley's XI against Boughton Park. He was also a useful bowler in the Birmingham League for Walsall, who won the league in 1893 with the help of his 68 wickets, including four in four balls against Wednesbury. The following season he took 9 for 20 at Sandwell Park against West Bromwich Dartmouth, but his best first-class figures were 7 for 41 in 1903 against Oxford University in their second innings, having taken 5 for 57 in the first. These, however, were not his best match figures as he had already taken 14 for 109 against Hampshire at Southampton in 1901. Nineteen wickets fell on the first day and rain prevented play on the second, as there were no pitch inspectors in those days. Bird finished off the Hampshire innings with the wicket of Henry Baldwin, finishing with 7 for 53. Worcestershire pressed on for a declaration and left the home side needing 220 runs to win, but Bird created havoc once again and they were all out in 43 overs for 129, with Bird taking 7 for 56.

When the Australians made their first visit to New Road in 1902, Worcestershire were well beaten by 174 runs but Bird had reason to be pleased with his performance. In the Australian first innings he took 6 for 69 and followed this with 2 for 40 in the second, but some indifferent Worcestershire batting in their second innings saw them collapse to 97 all out with Ernie Jones (6 for 53) and Warwick Armstrong (4 for 34) bowling unchanged.

In July 1902 against Lancashire, Bird joined Fred Wheldon with the eighth wicket having fallen at 295. Ninety-two runs later, on the second morning, Wheldon was bowled by the Aston Villa, Everton and England winger, Jack Sharp, and Bird went on to a career best 64*. He almost eclipsed this innings two seasons later when he scored 63* against Yorkshire at New Road in 1904. Following-on 236 runs behind, Worcestershire won thanks to an opening partnership of 176 by Fred Bowley (107) and Dick Pearson (66) and a 'backs to the wall' unbroken ninth wicket partnership of 71 with G.H.T. Simpson-Hayward, Bird doing almost all of the scoring.

Bird had a strong family sporting background. His brother, William, played second-class cricket for Warwickshire and his cousin, Jim Windridge, played cricket for Warwickshire and soccer for Birmingham. Bird died at the age of fifty-eight, after a long illness.

Ronnie Bird
RHB & RMF, 1946-54

Born: Quarry Bank, Staffordshire, 4 April 1915
Died: Feckenham, 20 February 1985

Batting career:

M	I	NO	Runs	Av	50
190	317	31	7445	36	36

100	Ct/St
7	150

Bowling career:

O	M	R	W	5wl	10wM
293	41	1110	23	-	-

Career best performances:
158* v. Somerset, Taunton, 1952
3-26 v. Northamptonshire, Worcester, 1948

Ronnie Bird did not make his first-class debut until he was thirty-one, owing to the Second World War. Like so many others, he lost five seasons of opportunity between 1939 and 1945. When the Indians visited New Road in 1946 Bird, after a long wait, was in the Worcestershire line-up.

The former Worcestershire cricketer, the Nawab of Pataudi, led the Indians, won the toss, asked the home side to bat and Bird had the misfortune to be bowled by Sadashiv Shinde before he had scored, the first of the leg-spinner's 39 wickets on the tour. Shinde had five more wickets in the second innings, including Bird, caught and bowled for 3, but Worcestershire ran out winners by 16 runs. By the end of the season things had improved for Bird and he finished his first season with a creditable 801 runs at an average of 20.53 with three half-centuries, the best of them 72* at New Road against Leicestershire, where he shared a ninth wicket partnership of 61 with Roly Jenkins.

Horsham was the venue of the first of his 7 centuries, when he scored 105 and shared a sixth wicket partnership of 105, again with Jenkins, which led to a first innings lead of 105. Jenkins' share was 63 and with match figures of 10 for 157 he gave Worcestershire a chance to force a win. This was achieved with just three minutes remaining thanks to an enterprising partnership between Don Kenyon and Alan White of 77 for the second wicket.

Three times during his nine seasons with Worcestershire he completed 1,000 runs, with a best of 1,591 at an average of 37.00 in 1952, having been appointed captain during the winter, and his three centuries included his career best. Worcestershire were given a good start by Kenyon and Peter Richardson at Taunton, with 104 for the first wicket, but a collapse left them at 111 for 5 when Jenkins again helped Bird to add 82 for the sixth. Martin Horton then gave good support in a seventh wicket stand of 115 and when Bird declared at 358 for 9, he had hit a five and 16 fours and was 158*. It was another good match for Jenkins, who took 4 for 33 and 6 for 64 and Somerset were well beaten by an innings and 54 runs. Bird captained Worcestershire 112 times, leading the side to 30 wins and 38 draws before his retirement from regular first-class cricket at the end of 1954, to be replaced by Reg Perks.

Before the Second World War he was a professional with Warwickshire and played Birmingham League cricket for Moseley, for whom he scored 157* against Old Hill at Haden Hill in 1939. All his first-class cricket was for Worcestershire except for five appearances for the MCC.

Roy Booth
RHB & WK, 1956-70

Born: Marsden, Yorkshire, 1 October 1926

Batting career:

M	I	NO	Runs	Av	50
402	594	107	9360	19.21	23
14	*12*	*2*	*160*	*16.00*	*-*

100	Ct/St
2	868/147
-	*28/2*

Bowling career:

O	M	R	W	5wI	10wM
2	0	3	0	-	-

Career best performances:

113* v. Sussex, Hove, 1959
55 v. Nottinghamshire, Worcester, 1968

Roy Booth spent six seasons on the Yorkshire staff but was never a regular member of the First XI apart from in 1954, when he played in all the County Championship matches and seven other first-class matches, scoring 384 runs at an average of 14.22, holding 37 catches and taking 19 stumpings. The following season he shared wicketkeeping duties with Jimmy Binks but joined Worcestershire for the 1956 season.

Hugo Yarnold had retired at the end of the 1955 season, so Booth immediately took over his duties and was present in all their matches and was capped that season, distinguishing himself with 62 dismissals. His debut was against the Australian tourists, when he was leg before to Ray Lindwall before he had scored. He scored his maiden first-class century at Hove in 1959 when he shared a sixth wicket partnership of 111 with 'Laddie' Outschoorn, hitting 16 fours. At the end of the season he was just six runs short of his 1,000 runs for the side, although an innings of 48 for the MCC against Yorkshire at Scarborough in September took him past four figures for the first, and only, time.

At the end of the 1960 season he completed a record 100 dismissals, with 85 catches and 16 stumpings, but was 64 short of 1,000 runs. Three of these stumpings were in the infamous match at Tunbridge Wells when Worcestershire were beaten by an innings and 101 runs in a day. Two of these stumpings were off debutant Norman

Gifford and the other off Doug Slade, but Worcestershire's first innings of 25 lasted only one hour and thirty-five minutes and the second of 61 took just an hour and forty minutes. In the match before this defeat, they met Lancashire at Old Trafford. Worcestershire followed-on 214 runs behind but an unbroken eighth wicket partnership of 113 with Derek Pearson saved the game, with Booth left on 99*.

The 1962 season ended with Booth having taken 97 dismissals for Worcestershire and scored another century, but this was the first time that he had topped the national wicketkeeper dismissals list. He shone with the bat at Old Trafford with a 102* that included a six and 11 fours in three and a half hours. During this season he also had his best match behind the stumps when he held three catches in the Essex first innings at Romford and five in the second. This second innings performance equalled his best innings performance, something he achieved on nine different occasions during his career.

During Worcestershire's 1964 County Championship campaign, Booth became the last wicketkeeper to take 100 dismissals in a season when he held 90 catches and took 10 stumpings. An hour and a quarter after Booth had stumped Ken Graveney off Gifford, Worcestershire were crowned champions when

Worcestershire v. Gloucestershire. David Allen, Roy Booth, Dick Richardson and Alan Spencer.

news came through that Hampshire had beaten Warwickshire.

In 1963 the one-day knock-out competition began and Booth played in the first of these finals. Worcestershire met Sussex at Lord's in the Gillette Cup final. Batting second in poor light, Booth caused Sussex problems when he shared a last wicket partnership of 21 with Bob Carter. Carter was run out with eight balls remaining and 15 runs required to win with Booth 33*. In 1968, they returned to Lord's for the final and this time were beaten by their neighbours Warwickshire by five wickets. His best performance in this competition was at New Road in 1968, when he scored 55 and shared a sixth wicket partnership of 71 with his captain, Tom Graveney. These performances, however, were overshadowed by an all round match-winning performance of 95* and 4 for 15 by Gary Sobers, the Nottinghamshire captain.

During the winter of 1964/65, Booth went on tour with Worcestershire, playing two first-class matches against Rhodesia, winning one and losing the other. They won the Championship again in 1965 and began a tour of Jamaica in March 1966. Booth kept wicket against a Jamaican XI, the tour's only first-class fixture.

When the Championship success of 1965 is talked of, the last match of the season is high on the list of topics. Worcestershire went to Hove on the back of six successive victories and a seventh would give them the title. They were in trouble when Basil D'Oliveira was leg-before to Alan Oakman, with the score at 70-5 and 61 more runs required to win. Booth had joined Dick Richardson and together they added a crucial 51 runs before Booth was dismissed by John Snow for 38, with eleven runs still needed. Richardson and Slade successfully managed these runs and the match and a second Championship title were won.

Booth retired at the end of the 1968 season, the only Worcestershire wicketkeeper to take in excess of 1,000 dismissals, and he is twelfth in the list headed by Bob Taylor. An injury to Rodney Cass during the 1970 season found Booth being recalled to the side, making his debut in the Sunday League. He played his only game in this competition at Folkestone at the age of 43 years and 305 days, one of only nine cricketers to play in the League who had been born in the 1920s. Booth was a Worcestershire committee member from 1969 until 1999 and in February 1999 he was elected president.

Ian Botham OBE
RHB & RM, 1987-91

Born: Heswall, Cheshire, 24 November 1955

Batting career:

M	I	NO	Runs	Av	50
54	75	6	2097	30.39	10
77	69	10	2100	35.59	10

100	Ct/St
4	36
3	37

Bowling career:

O	M	R	W	Av	5wI	10wM
1105	224	3372	131	25.74	5	1
604.3	57	2654	119	22.30		-

Career best performances:

161 v. West Indies, Worcester, 1991

138 v. Gloucestershire, Bristol, 1990

7-54 v. Warwickshire, Worcester, 1991

5-27 v. Gloucestershire, Gloucester, 1987

Ian Botham joined Worcestershire in 1987 after an extremely successful career with Somerset and England. At the end of this first season the side had won the Sunday League title, as it did in 1988 together with the County Championship. A further Championship title was won in 1989 and in 1991 Worcestershire won their first Lord's one-day final when they beat Lancashire.

The first of these successes, the Sunday League in 1987, was achieved with the help of some fine opening stands with Tim Curtis. Botham and Curtis opened together on nine occasions, adding 655 runs at an average of 72.77 with four partnerships in excess of 100. The much heralded return to Taunton was ruined by rain but not before Botham had scored 126* from 111 balls with 3 sixes and 16 fours. With Phil Neale he added an unbroken 197 in 36 overs, the best for the fifth wicket for Worcestershire against Somerset.

The following season he suffered a serious back injury after four matches and missed the rest of the ssummer, but his interest and enthusiasm were high throughout and the confidence he gave his colleagues providing morale-boosting encouragement was immense. He returned for the start of the 1989 season and appeared in 12 Championship matches, including his only ten-wickets-in-a-match performance for the county. At Northampton he had 6 for 99 in the first innings and 5 for 76 in the second in an innings win and finished the season with 53 wickets at an average of 22.18 – his best season with the ball and an important contribution to a second Championship title.

During his last season with Worcestershire in 1991 he hit two centuries and had his best season for them with the bat, scoring 728 runs. Against the West Indian tourists he hit 161 and once again he shared a century stand with Neale, this time one of 136 for the fifth wicket. It was vintage Botham, his hundred coming off 83 balls. When he was out, he had faced just 139 balls and hit a six and 32 fours.

The challenge that Durham offered Botham when they joined the County Championship in 1992 was taken up and he stayed there until his eventual retirement towards the end of the 1993 season. He left with 19,399 runs, with 38 centuries, and 1,172 wickets in all first-class cricket and with 102 Test caps, 5,200 runs and 383 wickets. Many thousands of pounds have been raised from his monumental charity walks and for some time now he has been a highly respected member of the television commentary team.

Fred Bowley

RHB, 1899-1923

Born: Brecon, Wales, 9 November 1873						
Died: Worcester, 31 May 1943						

Batting career:

M	I	NO	Runs	Av	50	
396	722	24	20750	29.72	97	
100	Ct/St					
38	144					

Bowling career:

O	M	R	W	Av	5wl	10wM
21	0	101	4	25.25	-	-

Career best performances:

276 v. Hampshire, Dudley, 1914

1-6 v. Sussex, Hove, 1900

Fred Bowley first played for Worcestershire in 1894, prior to them achieving first-class status, and he was a regular member of their successful Minor Counties side between 1895 and 1898. However, his cricketing skills were first noticed as a teenager with Derbyshire Colts and Heanor Cricket Club. His first-class debut was in Worcestershire's first away match at Hove in May 1899 and his last was on that same South Coast, but this time at Southampton twenty-four years later, his only appearance in the 1923 season.

During his second season he became the first Worcestershire professional to make 1,000 runs in a season, reaching this target on thirteen further occasions, a club record until Don Kenyon overtook him in 1962 with his fifteen. At New Road in May 1900, he scored the first of his 38 hundreds, with 118 in just over four and a half hours against Hampshire. Three of these hundreds were made in two doubles, with 217 in the first ever first-class fixture at Stourbridge in 1905. Ted Arnold joined Bowley at the fall of the third wicket and four hours later they had added 216, a record for the fourth wicket for Worcestershire against Leicestershire.

In 1913 Bowley took part in another partnership that is still in the Worcestershire record books for the match against Gloucestershire at New Road when he added 306 for the first wicket with Dick Pearson. Bowley scored 201 in three and a half hours with 27 fours in what is still the best opening stand for Worcestershire against Gloucestershire.

His third, and final, double century was scored in June 1914 at Dudley against Hampshire and was the highest by a Worcestershire batsman until beaten by Glenn Turner in 1982. He hit 276 in four hours and fifty minutes, with 2 sixes, a five and 33 fours, reaching his hundred before lunch on the first day, an achievement he reached on six occasions during his career. This innings will never be beaten at Dudley because the Tipton Road ground has disappeared and is now a business park and hotel site.

Bowley was followed by many great openers, Kenyon and Turner included, but the opening partnership that he shared with Harry Foster against Derbyshire at Derby in 1901 is still the Worcestershire record for a first wicket. They were together for three hours and ten minutes and added 309, with Bowley first out for 140, and Foster, a run later, for 152.

Glamorgan hired him as their coach on a three year contract when he left Worcestershire early in the 1923 season, and he later coached at Repton, Haileybury and St Paul's schools.

Brian Brain

RHB & RFM, 1959-75

Born: Worcester, 13 September 1940

Batting career:

M	I	NO	Runs	Av	50
149	157	41	807	6.95	-
101	*53*	*23*	*253*	*8.43*	-

100	Ct/St
-	33
-	*18*

Bowling career:

O	M	R	W	Av	5wl	10wM
4163.3	750	12298	508	24.20	20	5
846.1	*113*	*3048*	*143*	*21.31*	-	-

Career best performances:

38 v. Gloucestershire, Cheltenham, 1964

21* v. Sussex, Worcester, 1967

8-55 v. Essex, Worcester, 1975

4-13 v. Durham, Ropery Lane, Chester-le-Street, 1968

Brian Brain first played for Worcestershire's Second XI as a sixteen year old in 1957, after a promising school career with King's School, Worcester. He made his debut two years later at New Road against Oxford University and had figures of 3 for 35 and 2 for 54. His first wicket was that of Javed Burki, the future Pakistani Test cricketer, caught by Roy Booth. After one Second XI game in 1960 he was lost to Worcestershire cricket, until his return to the Second XI for three matches during the 1963 season when they won the Second XI Championship. The following season he played in eight matches in the county's successful 1964 season and in his first match of the season, only his second in the Championship, he had figures of 6 for 93 in the Somerset first innings at the Imperial Services Ground, with 4 for 73 in the second. At the end of the season he had taken 31 wickets at an average of 24.19, 30 of them in the Championship. For the Second XI he had taken a Worcestershire record of 81 wickets at 15.54 in sixteen Second XI Championship matches.

He became a first team regular, taking 73 wickets in 1969 and 84 in both the 1973 and 1974 seasons, the latter being Worcestershire's third County Championship title success. He had his career best figures during his last season when he had match-winning figures of 8 for 55 in the Essex second innings at New Road, having taken 3 for 52 in the first.

Brain played in the second of Worcestershire's Gillette Cup final defeats when they were beaten by Warwickshire. Norman Gifford and Brain shared an eighth wicket of 50, which remained the Worcestershire best for this wicket in the competition until it was beaten in the first match of the 2000 'series' against Gloucestershire by Ryan Driver and Richard Illingworth. Owing to an incredible administrative error, this match had to be replayed, as Kabir Ali, who took wickets in this first match, was appearing illegally.

At the end of the 1975 season, Brain was released along with Rodney Cass, Keith Wilkinson and Jim Yardley, a decision that forced the committee to arrange a meeting at the City's Guildhall. The room was too small to accommodate the complaining members, so another meeting was arranged in Malvern, but sadly Brain left and spent six successful seasons with Gloucestershire, taking 316 wickets at 24.98 with a best of 7 for 51 at Bristol against the 1977 Australians.

In 1981, with the help of Pat Murphy, Brain published a book titled *Another Day, Another Match*, the diary of a county cricketer's season.

Bob Broadbent
RHB & RMF, 1950-63

Born: Beckenham, Kent, 21 June 1924
Died: Callow End, Worcestershire, 26 April 1993

Batting career:

M	I	NO	Runs	Av	50
307	520	56	12800	27.58	70
4	*3*	*0*	*64*	*21.33*	*1*

100	Ct/St
13	297
-	*2*

Bowling career:

O	M	R	W	Av	5wl	10wM
96	13	382	4	95.50	-	-

Career best performances:

155 v. Middlesex, Worcester, 1951
1-16 v. Surrey, Kidderminster, 1952
51 v. Glamorgan, Neath, 1963

On leaving Caterham School, Broadbent joined the RAF as a seventeen year old, was trained in Canada as a navigator and saw operational service in the Far East. At twenty-two he was demobilised and went into banking. He joined Worcestershire at the end of the 1950 after a handful of Minor Counties appearances for Middlesex in 1949, and immediately made an impression in the last match of the season, with 77 and 29* against Leicestershire at Grace Road. During the first innings he shared partnerships of 88 with Don Kenyon for the fifth wicket and 66 with Dick Howorth for the sixth. And from then until his last season he very rarely missed a match and scored more than 1,000 runs in a season seven times.

Broadbent seemed to save his better performances for matches against his former county, Middlesex, and finished with an aggregate of 1,005 runs at 31.40 against them, including 6 fifties and one century, his career best being 155 at New Road in 1951. He was at the wicket for five and a quarter hours, hit 2 sixes and 22 fours and shared two century partnerships. The first was of 132 with his skipper Ronnie Bird for the fifth wicket and one of 115 for the sixth with Eddie Cooper, helping Worcestershire to 436 for 9 declared and an eventual ten wickets win. This century, and two others that season, plus some splendid close-to-the-wicket catching, led to the award of his county cap. His catching prowess made headlines at Stourbridge in 1960 when he caught six second innings Glamorgan batsmen, a Worcestershire record. With one taken in their first innings, he finished one short of the Worcestershire match record of nine, taken by William Burns in 1907 at Bradford.

The best of his 48 century partnerships was shared with George Dews at New Road, against the Combined Services in 1951. They added 248 for the fourth wicket in three hours against an attack including LAC Alan Moss, Sgmn Brian Close and AC Fred Titmus. Two partnerships of 167 are his best in the Championship, the first with Ronnie Bird for the fourth wicket at Eastbourne in 1952 and then in 1957, for the second, with Kenyon against Nottinghamshire at New Road.

His 1961 benefit cheque of £5,481 was invested in a partnership with Bob Mann, forming the Mann Broadbent Insurance Services. This was soon well established, with an emphasis initially on sport.

George Brook

RHB & SLA, 1930-35

Born: Mirfield, Yorkshire, 30 August 1888
Died: Bournemouth, Hampshire, 24 July 1966

Batting career:

M	I	NO	Runs	Av	50
150	218	17	1877	9.33	3

100	Ct/St
-	77

Bowling career:

O	M	R	W	Av	5wI	10wM
4157	692	12841	461	27.85	23	4

Career best performances:

56 v. Gloucestershire, Worcester, 1933
7-50 v. Leicestershire, Leicester, 1930

George Brook came to the Midlands after playing for Keighley in the Bradford League to join Kidderminster as their professional for 1929 in the Birmingham League. His 80 wickets helped them to their first title for five years. Twice he took 8 wickets in an innings, with 8 for 25 at Smethwick and 8 for 55 at home against Aston Unity. In the match at Chester Road against Moseley he took five wickets and scored 62 and the collection for him that day raised £6. These exploits interested Worcestershire and he joined them in 1930, informing them that he was thirty-four. The 1975 and 1976 editions of *Wisden* record different dates of birth – in the former, his year of birth is given as 1895 while the 1976 edition has the correct year, 1888. He was, therefore, forty-one when he made his debut at New Road against the Australian tourists, bowling 36 overs for 148 runs with the wickets of Bill Woodfull, Archie Jackson, Stan McCabe and Don Bradman. Woodfull scored 133, Bradman, in his first innings in England, 236, and they shared a second wicket partnership of 208 in two hours and ten minutes. By the end of this first season he had taken 132 wickets, 128 of them in the Championship, with twelve of five-in-an-innings performances and two of ten-in-a-match. His best of the season, 7 for 50 in the second innings against Leicestershire at

Aylestone Road, in a low scoring game which Worcestershire won by 43 runs, remained a career best. In the first innings he had taken 5 for 40 and his 12 for 90 were also his career best match figures.

The first of his three half-centuries was at Cheltenham in 1932. Coming in with the Worcestershire score at 47 for 7, he joined Bernard Quaife and they added 72 for the eighth wicket, with Brook's share 54. Later in the season he just beat this by being 54* at Hinckley when Cyril Walters declared the Worcestershire innings on 502 for 9 in a drawn match against Leicestershire. His career best was hit the following season, when Gloucestershire were the visitors to New Road. Worcestershire were chasing a total of 541 and Brook joined Quaife, once more at the fall of the seventh wicket, and they added 70, of which Brook scored 56.

By 1935 Dick Howorth had taken over the slow left-armer's spot in the side and Brook made only three appearances. He left at the end of the season to rejoin Keighley, later turning out for Bowling Old Lane, who were also in the Bradford League.

Charlie Bull

RHB, 1931-39

Born: Lewisham, Kent, 29 March 1909
Died: Margaretting, Essex, 28 May 1939

Batting career:

M	I	NO	Runs	Av	50
171	302	20	6768	24.00	30

100	Ct/St
5	62

Bowling career:

O	M	R	W	Av	5wI	10wM
7.2	0	56	0	-	-	-

Career best performances:
161 v. Glamorgan, Cardiff, 1934

Charlie Bull joined Worcestershire having played four matches in two seasons with Kent. He made his debut in 1931 against the New Zealanders at New Road. A qualifying period was spent with Dudley in the Birmingham League in 1932, scoring 606 runs including 107* in an unbroken first-wicket partnership of 264 with Leslie Gale against Aston Unity. Regular county cricket followed in 1933 as he appeared in 23 of the 30 Championship matches, scoring 743 runs at an average of 21.85. His first century, 161 against Glamorgan at Cardiff in 1934, was to be his career best, hitting 24 fours and sharing a sixth wicket partnership of 124 with Dick Howorth in 115 minutes.

At The Bat and Ball Ground, Gravesend in 1933, Bull shared in his best partnership for Worcestershire. He was very much the junior in a stand of 260 for the fourth wicket in three hours, scoring just 79 of them with his partner, Cyril Walters, who went on to a career best of 226. At Kidderminster in 1935 he carried his bat through the 195 minutes of the his side's first innings against Lancashire, scoring 57 not out during a total of 150. Following-on 225 runs behind, 'Doc' Gibbons then carried his bat for 83* but Lancashire left Chester Road with an innings and 77 runs victory. Bull hit one century during this season, 118 at Edgbaston, which helped Worcestershire to a healthy total of 365 and their first win over Warwickshire since 1925. He shared an opening partnership of 133 in 135 minutes with Gibbons when play finally started after lunch on the first day due to rain, and another of 109 for the fifth wicket with Frank Warne. His innings lasted 345 minutes and he hit 5 fours. He was finally bowled by Jimmy Ord for the last of Ord's two wickets in first-class cricket.

Following his best season's aggregate, 1,619 runs in 1937, Bull opened against the 1938 Australians at New Road, but in attempting a hook of one of the 35 no-balls bowled by Ernie McCormick, he had to retire hurt. He was already nursing a broken finger and this, together with the blow on the head, kept him out for nine games. When he retuned he found it difficult to make runs and his aggregate for the season was 497 runs at an average of 21.60.

Back to full fitness for 1939, he still found runs hard to get and had scored 121 runs in 10 innings when Worcestershire went to Chelmsford for the annual Whitsuntide fixture with Essex. After fielding all day to an Essex total of 275, Bull and Syd Buller were involved in a motor accident at Margaretting, between Billericay and Chelmsford, on the Saturday evening. Tragically, Bull was killed and Buller seriously injured.

Born: Upper Wortley, Leeds, Yorkshire, 23
August 1909

Died: Edgbaston, Birmingham, 7 August 1970

Batting career:

M	I	NO	Runs	Av
10	168	43	1732	13.85
50	100	Ct/St		
2	-	176/71		

Career best performances:

64 v. Northamptonshire, Kettering, 1938

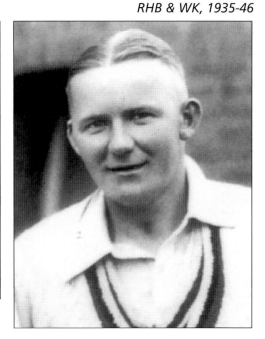

Syd Buller joined Worcestershire having been at Yorkshire playing Minor Counties cricket since 1929 and league cricket with Bradford Park Avenue. During one of these matches for Yorkshire against Staffordshire at Walsall in August 1934, he spoke with Walsall captain, Maurice Foster, one of the Worcestershire brotherhood. The following season he began a qualifying period for Worcestershire, appearing in one first-class match against the touring South Africans on the opening day of 1935. He was bowled by Bob Crisp in the first innings and Alex Bell in the second, both times before he had scored and he had to wait until August 1936 before he made his County Championship debut at Edgbaston in a rain-affected game against Warwickshire. The following season he played in all the games until an injury at Lord's in July kept him out of the side for 4 matches. He finished the season with 62 dismissals, 18 of them stumpings. Buller had his best season in 1938, when he scored 585 runs and took 67 dismissals, again 18 of them stumpings. He hit a career best 64 at Kettering against Northamptonshire, sharing a fifth wicket partnership of 97 with 'Doc' Gibbons.

On the Saturday evening of the Whitsuntide fixture at Chelmsford, Buller was injured in the motor accident in which Charlie Bull lost his life. He missed the next seventeen matches, coming back at the end of July for the return match with Essex at New Road.

War service with the RAF followed from 1942, until he was demobbed on Thursday 2 May 1946, appearing two days later for Worcestershire against the touring Indians. At the end of this season he retired, took over the coaching duties at New Road and umpired some of the Club and Ground matches. In 1951 he joined the first-class umpires list and stood in his first Test match in June 1956 at Trent Bridge, where Peter Richardson was making his debut against the Australians.

Buller was one of the central figures in the controversy over throwing in the 1960s, calling Geoff Griffin, the South African fast bowler. His partner, Frank Lee, called Griffin eleven times during the match, which finished early on the fourth day. An exhibition match was then staged, Buller called Griffin for throwing four times out of five and the unfortunate bowler finished the match bowling underarm.

Buller received the MBE for services to umpiring in June 1965, the first umpire to get this honour. On 7 August 1970 he died tragically, during a hold up for rain at Edgbaston where he was umpiring the Warwickshire versus Nottinghamshire match.

William Burns
RHB & RF, 1903-13

Born: Rugeley, Staffordshire, 29 August 1883
Died: Contalmaison, France, 7 July 1916

Batting career:

M	I	NO	Runs	Av	50
196	335	20	8688	27.58	44

100	Ct/St
12	132

Bowling career:

O	M	R	W	Av	5wl	10wM
1458.1	156	5752	187	30.75	5	1

Career best performances:

196 v. Warwickshire, Edgbaston, 1909
6-41 v. Somerset, Taunton, 1913

William Burns played Minor Counties cricket for Staffordshire in 1901 and 1902 and on his debut scored 123* against MCC and Ground at Lichfield, followed by a second innings nought and another innings of 123 against Oxfordshire in 1902. This was the end of his career with the county of his birth and in 1903 he was qualifying for Worcestershire as an amateur. He played in three matches that season, none of them in the Championship. The following season he was seen more regularly and hit the first of his 12 centuries with 165 at New Road against Oxford University, in a match that saw the University score 403 for the loss of 7 wickets off 91 overs, in four hours and five minutes, to win by three wickets.

He completed the first of his three 1,000 runs in a season in 1906 and during that season equalled his career best. Once again Oxford University suffered but this time Worcestershire did manage to win the match. In just over two hours he hit 25 fours, followed, nine matches later, by his first Championship hundred, 109 in an hour and three-quarters against Hampshire at Stourbridge. The next time he batted, he scored 125 at New Road against Warwickshire, sharing

a sixth wicket partnership of 166 with Harry Foster.

Edgbaston was the scene for his career best batting performance, when he scored 196 against Warwickshire in 1909. He hit 17 fours and, with Ted Arnold, added 393 for the fifth wicket – an English record for this wicket until beaten by Mal Loye and David Ripley for Northamptonshire in 1998.

During the winter of 1906/07 he toured New Zealand with the MCC, led by Captain Edward Wynyard, and he was also selected for the Gentlemen against the Players, at The Oval and Scarborough in 1910 and at Lord's the following season. In the Oval match he took 7 for 58 in the first innings, taking the last three Players' wickets in four balls.

Eleven all-rounders have scored a century and performed the hat-trick in the same match but Burns is the only Worcestershire cricketer amongst them. At New Road in 1913 he scored 103* in an innings of 529 for 4 declared, hitting a five and 12 fours in under two hours against Gloucestershire and then dismissing Dipper, Nason and Barnett with successive balls.

At the end of the 1913 season he settled in Canada, but returned to England to enlist in the First World War. A Second Lieutenant in the Worcestershire Regiment, he was killed in action on 7 July 1916.

Dick Burrows
RHB & RF, 1899-1919

Born: Eastwood, Nottinghamshire, 6 June 1871
Died: Eastwood, Nottinghamshire, 12 February 1943

Batting career:

M	I	NO	Runs	Av	50
277	436	65	5523	14.07	9

100	Ct/St
2	138

Bowling career:

O	M	R	W	Av	5wI	10wM
6814.5	1049	23604	894	26.40	57	9

Career best performances:

112 v. Gloucestershire, Worcester, 1907
8-48 v Somerset, Taunton, 1908

Dick Burrows joined Worcestershire before their first-class days in 1893. He assisted Stourbridge in the Birmingham League as their professional between 1894 and 1897, taking nine Aston Unity wickets at Stourbridge during his first season. When Worcestershire opened their first County Championship season in 1899 against Yorkshire at New Road, he was in the side and played in every match that season, taking 53 wickets at an average of 22.69. Retiring after the short 1919 season, he had managed 17 seven-wickets-in-an-innings performances and, at that time, only Ted Arnold had taken more wickets for the county.

The best of these seven-in-an-innings figures was his 8 for 48 at Taunton in 1908 during the Somerset second innings, when they were dismissed for 77 with Burrows bowling 14.1 unchanged overs and Worcestershire winning comfortably by an innings in two days. When at his best, Burrows bowled quite quickly and proof of this was displayed when he bowled Archie MacLaren at Old Trafford in 1901, the bail allegedly travelling sixty-four yards and six inches. He returned there ten years later and bowled Bill Huddleston, the bail this time dispatched some sixty-seven yards and six inches.

The first of Burrow's two centuries, 112 at New Road against Gloucestershire in 1907, still has pride of place in the Worcestershire record books. He joined Jack Cuffe with the score at 254-8 and 181 runs later was caught by Jessop off Dennett, having hit 19 fours and shared in what is still Worcestershire's best ninth wicket partnership. His second century was hit during the last season prior to the First World War when, again against Gloucestershire at New Road, in 1914, he was unbeaten on 107 in Worcestershire's only innings in a drawn match.

Burrows' best match figures were achieved at Liverpool in 1905, when he took 13 Lancashire wickets for 205, 7 for 117 in the first innings and 6 for 88 in the second. At the end of seasons 1910 and 1913 he had taken exactly 100 wickets, having been four short of this target in 1901.

He appeared in six of the nine first-class matches that Worcestershire played in 1919, all of them two-day friendlies, taking the last of his 'five fours' at Bath with 5 for 57 against Somerset. After his retirement, he joined the first-class umpires list from 1924 until 1937, standing in one Test match with Frank Chester at Trent Bridge in 1926 where only fifty minutes play was possible.

Bob Carter
LHB & RFM, 1961-72

Born: Horden, County Durham, 11 July 1937

Batting career:

M	I	NO	Runs	Av	50
177	163	94	317	4.59	-
48	*15*	*10*	*20*	*4.00*	-
100	Ct/St				
-	54				
-	*2*				

Bowling career:

O	M	R	W	Av	5wl	10wM
4838.1	913	13630	521	26.16	17	2
380.1	*44*	*1423*	*62*	*22.95*	-	-

Career best performances:

23 v. Leicestershire, Leicester, 1975

7-61 v. Yorkshire, Dudley, 1971

5 v. Surrey, Worcester, 1963*

5-27 v. Sussex, Hove, 1971

Former school teacher Bob Carter made his first-class debut for Worcestershire against Oxford University at New Road in 1961 and took four of the first five second innings wickets for eight runs, finishing with figures of 4 for 46, his only appearance of the season. At the end of his first full season he had taken 70 championship wickets at an average of 22.07, including the first of his five-in-an-innings performances when he took 5 for 55 at Edgbaston. His early days at Worcester were spent in the shadows of Jack Flavell and Len Coldwell but, during the title winning seasons of 1964 and 1965, whenever they were away on Test match duty he provided excellent cover. He had 40 wickets at 20.92 in 1964 and 30 at 21.36 the following season, during which time he received his county cap. During 1965 he came into the side for the injured Coldwell at New Road against Lancashire and took the last six wickets for 7 runs in 25 balls, including the hat-trick: Ken Howard and Tom Greenough both caught, Roy Booth and Keith Goodwin bowled. His final second innings figures were 4.1-2-7-6, with Lancashire all out for 55.

Worcestershire got to the first Lord's one-day final in 1963 and were beaten by Sussex in what was then the Gillette Cup. Carter was in the Worcestershire line-up and as the light deteriorated joined Booth at the fall of the ninth wicket with 36 runs required to win. He defended stubbornly and helped add 21 for the last wicket before he was run out, with ten balls left and 15 runs short of an epic win. This is still Worcestershire's best last wicket partnership in any of their nine Lord's finals.

When Worcestershire won the first of their Sunday League titles in 1971, Carter missed only one match. At Hove in June he took 5 for 27, his best figures in the competition, and he finished the season with 20 wickets at 22.10. The same season, at Dudley, he had his career best first-class figures when he took 7 for 61 against Yorkshire – this was the last first-class match at this venue, which is now a building site being prepared for a business park and multi-screen cinema.

After leaving during the 1972 season, he played once for the MCC against Kent at Canterbury in 1973, taking the wicket of Colin Cowdrey in each innings and he then went into coaching. He was national coach on the ECB staff based at Edgbaston until 1999.

Frank Chester
LHB & SLA, 1912-14

Born: Bushey, Hertfordshire, 20 January 1895
Died: Bushey, Hertfordshire, 8 April 1957

Batting career:

M	I	NO	Runs	Av	50
54	90	17	1768	24.21	4

100	Ct/St
4	25

Bowling career:

O	M	R	W	Av	5wI	10wM
836.2	165	2493	80	31.16	2	-

Career best performances:

178* v. Essex, Colchester, 1914
6-43 v. Hampshire, Southampton, 1913

A passage from Frank Chester's 1956 autobiography *How's That* explains how he came to be a Worcestershire cricketer. 'I had been spotted by Alec Hearne, the famous Kent all-rounder, batting for Bushey and he recommended me for a trial at Worcester. So I left school, changed my knickerbockers for long trousers, packed my cheap green-cloth cap and, with my father, presented myself at Worcester.

Ted Arnold leaned against the net post while I batted for a few minutes, and called over his shoulder to H.K. Foster, the captain, and my father "He'll do"'. So Chester came to New Road to qualify in July 1910, playing for the Worcestershire Gentlemen and the Club and Ground, and made his first-class debut against the South African tourists in 1912. He struggled with the bat that season but showed promise with his slow left-armers, taking 26 wickets with a best of 4-53 at Catford against Kent. His first wicket was that of Wilfred Rhodes at Huddersfield, when he had him caught behind by Ernie Bale. Chester was quite proud of the congratulations that he received from George Hirst during the lunch interval.

During the 1913 season he hit three centuries, the first of them 115 at New Road against Somerset, at the age of 18 years and 158 days. He was the youngest Worcestershire batsman to score a century, but not as young as first thought.

For many years *Wisden* gave his date of birth as 1896, which would have made him seventeen in 1913, but Robert Brooke, joint founder of the Association of Cricket Statisticians, purchased his birth certificate and found this error. In the 1980 edition of *Wisden* his correct birth date is given. Centuries against Hampshire, 128* at Southampton, and Middlesex, 148* at Lord's followed, while at Southampton he completed a fine all-round performance with career-best figures of 6 for 43.

Then came the 1914 season, his last as a first-class cricketer. It was a slow start for him, but at New Road against Essex he hit a career best 178* and shared an unbroken partnership of 145 with W.H. Taylor, still the record for Worcestershire's eighth wicket against Essex. He finished the season 76 runs short of 1,000 runs but had little luck with the ball, taking just 16 wickets at 51.06.

In action in Salonika in July 1917, he lost his right arm below the elbow. His career was over, until he put a white coat over his hospital blue when convalescing at Roehampton and umpired a match at The Oval in 1918. So began a new career. He joined the first-class list in 1922 and by the time he had retired in 1955 had stood in 48 Test matches.

Len Coldwell
RHB & RFM, 1955-69

Born: Newton Abbot, Devon, 10 January 1933
Died: Teignmouth, Devon, 6 August 1996
Batting career:

M	I	NO	Runs	Av	50
296	333	92	1,446	6.00	-
17	*11*	*6*	*28*	*5.60*	*-*

100	Ct/St				
-	85				
-	*4*				

Bowling career:

O	M	R	W	Av	5wI	10wM
8823	2328	21490	1029	20.88	57	7
162.2	*32*	*463*	*23*	*20.13*	*-*	*-*

Career best performances:

37 v. Nottinghamshire, Worcester, 1962
8 v. Sussex, Worcester, 1967
8-38 v. Surrey, Worcester, 1965
4-39 v. Hampshire, Worcester, 1966

Len Coldwell came to Worcester by way of Minor Counties cricket for Devon and made his first-class debut at Oxford against the University in 1955, playing in another three matches that season. Reg Perks retired at the end of that season and Coldwell became Jack Flavell's regular new ball partner, forming a highly successful double act. Coldwell took eight wickets in an innings on four occasions, all at home, with two at New Road and one each at Dudley and Kidderminster. Worcestershire have never had a bowler take all ten wickets in a first-class match but during the last of these eight wickets performances, at New Road, Coldwell came very close. He had taken the first eight Surrey wickets for 11 runs – Geoff Arnold was dropped first ball and Roger Harman was also missed – but he had the satisfaction of his career best 8 for 38. Worcestershire won the match by an innings, Coldwell taking 2 for 45 in the second innings, and they went to Bournemouth and Hove to record two wins and take the County Championship title for the second season running.

In the two Championship-winning seasons he took 85 and 80 wickets but in 1961 and 1962 he took 140 and 139 respectively, his best performances over a season. Following the latter season he was chosen to tour Australia and New Zealand with Ted Dexter's England party, appearing in the Second and Third Test Matches, but with little success. Coldwell had made his Test debut in the summer before this tour and had his best figures of 6 for 85 in the Pakistan second innings at Lord's, with first match figures of 9 for 111 – an encouraging debut. In all he played in 7 Tests and took 22 wickets at an average of 27.72.

At the end of the 1964 season, Coldwell went with Worcestershire on what was the first such tour by an English county, visiting seven different countries and travelling 34,000 miles. In the initial first-class match that they played, at Bulawayo against Rhodesia, Coldwell helped Worcestershire to a 196 runs win with figures of 5 for 18 and 5 for 26.

Coldwell's career came to a rather sudden end during the 1969 season, with eleven matches still to be played, when he joined Whitbread's back in Devon on a business appointment. In 1996 he was looking forward to an hip replacement to rid him of the pain that he had suffered since his playing days. Sadly, two weeks after he had been with friends and former colleagues at the Worcestershire Old Players' reunion he died suddenly, at the age of sixty-three.

Eddie Cooper
RHB, 1936-51

Born: Bacup, Lancashire, 30 November 1915
Died: Birmingham, 29 October 1968

Batting career:

M	I	NO	Runs	Av	50
249	442	28	13213	31.91	70

100	Ct/St
-18	97

Bowling career:

O	M	R	W	Av	5wl	10wM
9.2	1	44	0	-	-	-

Career best performances:

216* v. Hampshire, Dudley, 1939

Eddie Cooper played for his local club, Bacup, in the Lancashire League before qualifying for Worcestershire during the 1936 season, when he made just one appearance in the Parks against Oxford University. From then on he became a regular until he retired at the end of the 1951 season, beginning with 1,212 runs in the County Championship in 1937, an aggregate for a first season in the competition beaten only by Basil D'Oliveira and Maurice Nichol. His maiden century was scored at Northampton in the August of that season, where he hit a six and 13 fours in four hours, sharing partnerships of 110 with Frank Warne for the third wicket and 106 with Vernon Grimshaw for the fourth. He ended the season with 1,321 runs, the first of nine consecutive seasons that he reached four figures.

At Dudley in 1938 he scored the only double-century of his career, 216* against Warwickshire, batting for six and a half hours and hitting 16 fours. Again, he shared two three-figure partnerships, the first, 123 for the third wicket with 'Doc' Gibbons and the second, 245 with Sid Martin, for the fourth. This innings, 111 at Dudley against Lancashire and 104 at Loughborough against Leicestershire, helped him towards his 1,663 runs for the season, the best aggregate of his career.

The following season he carried his bat through the Worcestershire innings of 272 at Old Trafford with 104*, including a six and 6 fours in 285 minutes, aged just 23 years and 226 days – becoming at the time the youngest Worcestershire batsman to do this. He batted throughout an innings once more after the Second World War, when he scored 69 out of a total of 154 at Dudley against Warwickshire in 1951.

When Don Kenyon came on to the scene in 1946, he formed a highly dependable pairing with Cooper, sharing 15 century opening partnerships in five seasons. In the July of that reawakening summer after five blank years, he scored a century in each innings of the match at Kidderminster against Northamptonshire, with 191 in the first and 106* in the second.

Leaving at the end of the 1952 season to take up a coaching appointment at the Royal Naval College, Dartmouth gave him the opportunity to play in the Minor Counties competition with Devon for two seasons. From 1958 until his death he was coach at Bedford School.

Jack Cuffe
RHB & SLA, 1903-14

Born: Toowoomba, Queensland, Australia, 26 June 1880
Died: Burton-on-Trent, 16 May 1931

Batting career:

M	I	NO	Runs	Av	50
215	357	32	7404	22.78	39

100	Ct/St
4	124

Bowling career:

O	M	R	W	Av	5wI	10wM
6652	1404	18273	716	25.52	31	6

Career best performances:

145 v. Hampshire, Bournemouth, 1905
9-38 v. Yorkshire, Bradford, 1907

Jack Cuffe played for New South Wales at Sydney against Queensland in December 1902, his first and only first-class appearance in Australia. Moving to England, he joined Worcestershire for the 1903 season and signed on for Glossop in 1905. Glossop were then in the Second Division of the Football League, having been relegated form the top flight the previous season and Cuffe made 279 League appearances between 1905/06 and 1914/15.

His debut for Worcestershire was at Oxford, where he took three second innings wickets. Later in the season, against American tourists, the Philadelphians, he scored 91 and shared a sixth wicket partnership of 109 with another soccer player, George Gaukrodger. In 1907 at Bradford he had career best figures of 9 for 38 against Yorkshire, Worcestershire's best until equalled by yet another soccer player, Arthur Conway of Wolves, at Moreton-in-Marsh in 1914. At Bournemouth in 1910 he performed the hat-trick when he dismissed H.W.M. Yates, E.M. Sprot and H.C. McDonnell with successive balls in the first innings but a century by C.B. Fry in the second put Hampshire in the driving seat for a 143 runs win.

Dean Park, Bournemouth was a favourite venue for Cuffe as it was there that, five years earlier, in 1905, he had scored the best of his 4 centuries. In the first innings he hit 145 and shared partnerships of 122 with William Hutchings for the third wicket and 113 with Ted Arnold for the fourth, with Worcestershire eventually winning by five wickets in the last over within a minute of time.

Although he failed to reach three figures in 1911, his best being 78, he reached 1,000 runs and took his 100th wicket in the first first-class match at Dudley where Gilbert Jessop was leading Gloucestershire. Cuffe went in to the match with 90 wickets, and a career best match analysis of 14 for 115, 6 for 74 and 8 for 42 put him comfortably past three figures. Having reached his 1,000 runs in the first innings when he had scored 31, he became the second Worcestershire cricketer, after Ted Arnold, to complete the double. Cuffe played in the Lancashire League during the First World War after leaving Worcestershire at the end of the 1914 season. He was on the first-class umpires list between 1925 and 1927.

On 16 May 1931 Cuffe's body was taken out of the River Trent at Burton, twelve days after his appointment as coach at Repton. His death certificate stated 'death by drowning due to throwing himself in the river, suicide whilst temporarily insane. No post mortem'.

Jim Cumbes
RHB & RFM, 1972-81

Born: East Didsbury, Manchester, 4 May 1944					
Batting career:					
M	**I**	**NO**	**Runs**	**Av**	**50**
109	92	43	384	7.83	-
100	*39*	*24*	*77*	*5.13*	-
100	**Ct/St**				
-	16				
-	*18*				
Bowling career:					
O	**M**	**R**	**W**	**Av**	**5wI**	**10wM**
2816.4	564	7902	246	32.12	8	-
795.1	*72*	*3081*	*103*	*29.91*	*-*	*-*

Career best performances:

43 v. Sussex, Hove, 1980
14* v. Sussex, Eastbourne, 1978
6-24 v. Yorkshire, Worcester, 1977
4-23 v. Sussex, Hove, 1974

Jim Cumbes made his first-class debut in 1977 at New Road for Lancashire and his first wicket was Don Kenyon, who was caught by the former Bury goalkeeper, Ken Grieves, in a rain-affected match. Sadly, Cumbes' cricket suffered because of his 'bread and butter' career as a goalkeeper with a string of clubs, beginning with Runcorn in 1963, to whom he returned in 1977. In between he played for Tranmere Rovers, West Bromwich Albion, Aston Villa, Portland Timbers in the USA, Coventry City , Southport, Worcester City and Kidderminster. During his Villa career he appeared in 181 matches, one of them at Wembley, in a 1-0 League Cup final win over Norwich City in 1975.

After leaving Lancashire he played for Surrey in 1968 and 1969, returned to Lancashire for 1970 and 1971 and joined Worcestershire in 1972, having his best season for them in 1977. At New Road in July he dismissed George Sharp, Bishen Bedi, and had Jim Griffths leg before to finish off the Northamptonshire first innings with a hat-trick. Later in the season, in August, he had career best figures of 6 for 24 in the second innings to help Worcestershire to an innings win over Yorkshire, only their fifth by this margin in 105 matches.

There were very few batting moments to savour but one which was highly memorable took place at Old Trafford in the semi-final of the Benson & Hedges Cup in 1973. Worcestershire required nine runs to win off the last over and Rodney Cass scored a single off the first ball; Brian Brain hit a four and a two and was caught by Clive Lloyd off Peter Lee off the fourth. Last man Cumbes entered the fray, didn't score off the fifth and scrambled a single off the last ball to tie the scores. Worcestershire had taken, with the help of Norman Gifford's 5 for 42, all ten Lancashire wickets and won by dint of having lost fewer wickets.

His career best with the bat occurred during a nightwatchman performance at Hove in 1980, when he joined Alan Ormrod after the dismissal of Glenn Turner. He scored 43, defied the efforts of Imran Khan and Geoff Arnold on the second morning, and added 79 for the second wicket, before he was bowled by the first ball from slow left-armer Alan Willows.

On being released at the end of the 1981 season, he had a season with Warwickshire and became their commercial manager before moving back to Old Trafford in 1982, becoming Lancashire's chief executive.

Tim Curtis

RHB & LB, 1979-97

Born: Chichester, Kent, 15 January 1960					
Batting career:					
M	**I**	**NO**	**Runs**	**Av**	**50**
323	548	64	20155	41.64	100
293	*286*	*38*	*10109*	*40.76*	*83*
100	**Ct/St**				
43	182				
6	*86*				
Bowling career:					
O	**M**	**R**	**W**	**Av**	**5wI** **10wM**
145.5	17	662	11	60.18	- -
6	*1*	*31*	*2*	*15.50*	*-* *-*

Career best performances:

248 v. Somerset, Worcester, 1991
136* v. Surrey, The Oval, 1994
2-17 v. Oxford University, Oxford, 1991
1-6 v. Cumberland, Worcester, 1988

Tim Curtis made his debut for Worcestershire against the Sri Lankan tourists in 1979, his only appearance of the season, scoring 15 and 27 and bowling one over of leg-spin for two runs. University studies at Durham and Cambridge reduced his opportunities for Worcestershire but, after winning his 'blue' in the 1983 University match at Lord's, he became a regular member of the side. On returning to Fenner's the following season he scored his maiden century, 129 against Cambridge, sharing a second wicket partnership of 226 with Dipak Patel. At Wellingborough School in August he scored his first Championship hundred, with 124 off 321 balls, hitting 18 fours. In the last match of the season at The Oval he scored 105, which brought him to an aggregate 1,405 runs for the season, the first of his eleven 1,000 runs in a season performances.

In 1986 at Neath, he helped Graeme Hick add an unbroken 287 against Glamorgan, a Worcestershire Championship record for the second wicket. Curtis' share was 66* and their partnership lasted just 172 minutes, with Phil Neale declaring at 300 for 1. When Glamorgan were dismissed for 256 in their second innings, Worcestershire were left with 225 runs to win in 48 minutes plus 20 overs. Another fine innings

from Curtis, 63*, and another unbroken partnership, 115 for the fourth wicket in 32 overs with Neale, led to a 7 wickets win.

Consistency at the top of the innings was eventually rewarded with selection for the Headingley and Oval Tests against the West Indies in 1988. His first innings at this level came to an end when he was leg-before to Kenny Benjamin for 12; from his four innings he scored 69 runs at 17.25. He was recalled the following season after England had been beaten by the Australians in the first two Test matches and had the best of his nine visits to the crease, with 41 at Edgbaston in a match that was drawn after the loss of ten hours' play on the second and third days.

During this short two-season, five-Test career, Worcestershire were winning the County Championship; with an average of 42.77 in 1988 and 48.52 in 1989, Curtis was playing an important role. A Worcestershire record second-wicket partnership against Hampshire at New Road in the first innings eventually led to a 10 wickets win when, with Hick, he shared 276 runs in 77 overs. Curtis scored 131 off 277 balls and hit 12 fours. Including this match, Hick and Curtis still share five inter-county partnership records, beginning with the 258 at Lord's in 1987 and finishing with 232 against Surrey at New Road in 1991. Two of them, 264

Tim Curtis is presented with his supporters' 'Player of the Year' award for 1990 by Supporters' Association president, Betty Godfrey.

at Taunton and 193 at Grace Road, were shared in 1990 and all of them were for the second wicket. Somerset were his favourite opponents as he scored 1,980 runs at 50.76 against them, including his career best 248 out of 575 for 8 declared at New Road in 1991. After 501 balls and 27 fours, Curtis was caught behind off Jeremy Hallett, having hit the highest ever score by a Worcestershire captain. During this marathon he shared partnerships of 256 for the third wicket with David Leatherdale, 107 for the fourth with Rhodes and 100 for the seventh with Richard Illingworth.

Curtis took over the captaincy from Neale during that 1991 season and handed over to Tom Moody in 1995 after the defeat at the hands of Lancashire in the semi-final of the Benson & Hedges Cup. During his reign the Refuge Cup was won at Old Trafford at the end of 1991 and the NatWest Trophy at Lord's in 1994. He was sometimes unfairly criticised for his one-day batting, but his partnerships with Ian Botham and later Tom Moody were responsible for some fine starts in this shorter form of cricket.

When Curtis left Worcestershire he had shared 33 century partnerships in the Sunday League, a figure equalled only by Gooch. Twelve of them were with Moody, eight with Hick, six with Botham, two with Gavin Haynes and one each with Damian D'Oliveira, Gordon Lord, Neale, Steve Rhodes and Martin Weston.

Curtis scored two centuries in the Sunday League, the best of them 124 at Taunton in 1990. His best one-day performance was in the NatWest Trophy on the way to Worcestershire's Lord's success, when he scored 136* in a competition record unbroken third wicket partnership of 309 with Moody.

From the end of the 1983 season Curtis spent his close-season teaching at his old school, Worcester Royal Grammar, and when he finally called it a day at the end of the 1997 season, he spent the summers there too. His parents, who moved to Malvern with young Tim in 1963, are still regular visitors to New Road as they were when they were giving him their support during his career.

George Dews
RHB, 1946-61

Born: Ossett, Yorkshire, 5 June 1921

Batting career:

M	I	NO	Runs	Av	50
374	638	53	16671	28.49	90

100	Ct/St
20	353

Bowling career:

O	M	R	W	Av	5wI	10wM
41	2	202	2	101.00	-	-

Career best performances:

145 v. Combined Services, Worcester, 1951

1-31 v. Derbyshire, Worcester, 1954

George Dews joined Worcestershire for the first season after the Second World War and made an unforgettable debut at Old Trafford when he was dismissed first ball in each innings by Eric Price. In the first innings he was caught by Jack Ikin and in the second, leg before. Things didn't get any better in the next match when he again failed to score, this time falling leg before to Warwickshire's Jack Marshall at Dudley. In his next match he opened with Eddie Cooper against the RAF in a first-class fixture at New Road and he scored 78 whilst adding 130 for the first wicket. Sadly, he got another nought in his next match at Ebbw Vale and that was the end of his first season, 13 runs in six Championship innings. His winter work took him to Ayresome Park for Middlesbrough and he helped them to a First Division mid-table position before moving to join Plymouth Argyle.

Meanwhile, he had to rebuild his cricket career. Misfortune followed him again when, in his only appearance of the 1947 season, he was out for 0 and 1 against the Combined Services at New Road, so it was off to a winter at Home Park. He stayed with Plymouth until the end of the 1954/55 season, making 257 League appearances, and joined Walsall for one season, 1955/56, scoring once against Gillingham and leaving after ten games.

Dews found more consistency during the 1950 season, completing 1,000 runs – the first of eleven such seasons – received his county cap, and in July he scored his maiden century, against Hampshire at Dudley. He was 1* at the close of play on the second day and was 101* when Ronnie Bird declared, scoring exactly 100 runs before lunch. His career best was 145 at New Road against the Combined Services, adding 248 for the fourth wicket with Bob Broadbent. However, the best of his 17 Championship centuries was against Essex in 1953 at New Road when he scored 139.

Dews is also remembered for some superb fielding and his haul of 353 catches was a Worcestershire record at the time, overtaken later by Dick Richardson and Alan Ormrod. He was awarded a benefit in 1960 and left at the end of the 1961 season

Dews had a three year spell as professional with Dudley in the Birmingham League between 1962 and 1964 and was employed by British Steel at the Round Oak site in Brierley Hill.

Graham Dilley
LHB & RFM, 1987-92

Born: Dartford, Kent, 18 May 1959					
Batting career:					
M	I	NO	Runs	Av	50
52	48	22	500	19.23	-
51	*10*	*4*	*69*	*11.50*	*-*
100	**Ct/St**				
-	8				
-	7				
Bowling career:					
O	M	R	W	Av	5wI	10wM
1275	233	3942	171	23.05	13	1
441.4	*54*	*1656*	*73*	*22.68*	*-*	*-*

Career best performances:

45* v. Glamorgan, Worcester, 1990
25 v. Essex, Chelmsford, 1987
6-43 v. Leicestershire, Worcestershire, 1987
5-29 v. Middlesex, Lord's, 1988

Graham Dilley joined Worcestershire from Kent during the winter of 1986/87 at the same time that Ian Botham arrived amid a fanfare of publicity. His first game was at New Road against his former county and he dismissed Neil Taylor and Simon Hinks in his second over, before a third wicket partnership of 285 between Mark Benson and Chris Tavaré spoiled the script. They were his only wickets in the match.

During this 1987 season he made four appearances against Pakistan as part of a Test career that had begun in December 1979 at Perth and continued until the fourth Test at Old Trafford against Australia in 1989, his forty-first appearance. He had taken 138 wickets at an average of 29.76 with a best haul of 6 for 38 at Christchurch in the first of the series against New Zealand in February 1988. His best remembered batting exploits are when he shared an eighth wicket partnership of 117 in 80 minutes with Ian Botham at Headingley during the England second innings follow-on, a match won amazingly on the last day when Bob Willis took 8 for 43 and Australia were dismissed for 111, 19 runs short of victory.

That first Worcestershire season of 1987, when they finished ninth in the Championship, ended with Dilley taking 21 wickets at an average of 20.42 and playing a minor role in

their Sunday League success. The following season the county enjoyed their most successful year, winning the County Championship, the Sunday League and reaching the NatWest final. This visit to Lord's, where they met Middlesex, saw Dilley have his best one-day bowl for Worcestershire when he had figures of 5 for 29 off 12 overs, although man of the match, Mark Ramprakash, with 56, helped Middlesex to a 3 wickets win. In the championship Dilley took 34 wickets at 20.44 in nine matches, with a best of 5 for 46 at Trent Bridge, having taken 5 for 55 against them at New Road.

Dilley was a considerable force in 1989, despite turning out less than 100 per cent fit several times. At Old Trafford he had match figures of 10 for 124 with his match-winning second innings the most memorable. Overnight, Lancashire were 160 for 2, Dilley 0 for 73, needing 106 to win. Dilley produced one of his finest spells to take 5 for 21 and the game was won by 36 runs.

Three more seasons of struggle with his knee injury came to an end after just two games of the 1992 season without taking a wicket. He retired, and has since had several short-term appointments as a bowling coach but leaving an impressive record of 648 wickets at 26.84, 257 of them for Kent.

Basil D'Oliveira OBE
RHB & RM, 1964-80

Born: Signal Hill, Cape Town, South Africa, 4 October 1931

Batting career:

M	I	NO	Runs	Av	50
278	435	65	14120	38.16	71
180	*164*	*18*	*3637*	*24.91*	*18*

100	Ct/St
31	158
2	*43*

Bowling career:

O	M	R	W	Av	5wl	10wM
5007.4	1521	11103	445	24.95	17	2
1262.4	*166*	*4283*	*183*	*23.40*	*-*	*-*

Career best performances:

227 v. Yorkshire, Hull, 1974
102 v. Sussex, Hove, 1974
6-29 v. Hampshire, Portsmouth, 1968
5-26 v. Gloucestershire, Lydney, 1972

Basil D'Oliveira's life and cricketing future took a fairy tale change in a kind of 'log cabin to White House' pattern in 1960 when he joined Lancashire League club Middleton. They had decided not to re-engage Roy Gilchrist as their professional and negotiations with Wes Hall had broken down. By a strange coincidence the league's historian, John Kaye, received a letter from D'Oliveira seeking a cricket position in England and so he suggested that his own club, Middleton, take a chance on this cricketer from the Cape with an impressive record in South Africa for the St Augustine's club. The risk became good judgement when he finished his first season with 930 runs and 70 wickets. When he left to join Worcestershire he had scored 3,663 runs, at an average of 48.20, and taken 238 wickets at 14.87 in four seasons.

In those days it was necessary to spend a qualifying period with a county and D'Oliveira spent his with Kidderminster in the Birmingham League, scoring 706 runs and taking 43 wickets in 1964. He made his Worcestershire debut against Bobby Simpson's Australians at New Road and had Bill Lawry caught by Roy Booth for his first wicket. During his third match, he scored the first of his 31 centuries when he hit 101 against Oxford University at New Road in one hour and fifty

minutes. The County Championship title was won without his help, but when success was repeated in 1965 he scored 1,653 runs and took 37 wickets. That runs aggregate is the most ever scored by a Worcestershire batsman in a first season in Championship cricket and included six hundreds, one of them 106 at New Road against Essex on his debut. He added 183 for the fourth wicket with Tom Graveney and followed this with 163 in the next game at Brentwood in the return match.

In 1966, D'Oliveira was selected in the twelve for the Old Trafford Test match against the West Indians but had to wait until the next one, at Lord's, before he made his debut. He helped Jim Parks add 48 for the sixth wicket when Parks drove the ball, striking the heel of D'Oliveira and then hitting the wicket. Hall quickly removed a stump and D'Oliveira was run out in the most unfortunate of ways for 27. Forty-three further Tests followed, with tours to West Indies in 1967/68, Pakistan in 1968/69 and Australia and New Zealand in 1970/71. At The Oval, for the last Test in 1968, D'Oliveira was brought back after being left out of three Tests and recorded his highest score at this level with 158 against the Australians. When the tour party to South Africa for the winter was announced, there was no room for D'Oliviera, but when Tom Cartwright withdrew through injury, he

Left: Basil D'Oliveira gives a rather unusual cricket lesson. Right: The Benson & Hedges Cup final at Lord's in 1976. An injured D'Oliveira puts the ball past Alan Knott to score his 50.

was called up as his replacement and the rest is history. The tour was called off and South Africa disappeared from international cricket for over twenty-one years until they met India in November 1991 in a one-day international in Calcutta.

The best of D'Oliveira's 43 first-class hundreds was for Worcestershire, against Yorkshire at Hull in 1974. He batted for just over six hours, scoring 227, hitting 2 sixes and 28 fours, and shared an eighth wicket partnership of 125 with Norman Gifford. Worcestershire won by an innings and 83 runs, and went on to win the County Championship pennant at the end of the season. Only Don Kenyon, with scores of 238* and 259, has scored double centuries for Worcestershire against Yorkshire.

D'Oliveira had an important role in the club's one-day success, becoming the first Worcestershire cricketer to complete the Sunday League career double of 1,000 runs and 100 wickets after 102 matches in 1977. His aggregate of 2,137 runs in this competition included 100 at Byfleet against Surrey in the first of Worcestershire's record eleven ties and at Lydney in 1972 he took 5 for 26 against Gloucestershire.

In the Gillette/NatWest competition he shares the record six 'man of the match' awards with Tim Curtis and was in the losing 1966 final side. In the Benson & Hedges Cup he was in the losing Lord's sides of 1973 and 1976, both against Kent. In the last of these he was top scorer for Worcestershire with 50, using Glenn Turner as his runner following a damaged hamstring he received when chasing an overthrow towards the Nursery End.

A benefit was awarded him in 1975 and he received a handsome £27,400, a Worcestershire record at the time. He played his last match against Middlesex at New Road at the end of May in 1980, having already been appointed the county coach and playing in the Second XI. In a match at New Road against Northamptonshire in 1979, he played in the Second XI Championship with his son, Damian.

Damian D'Oliveira
RHB & RM/OB, 1982-95

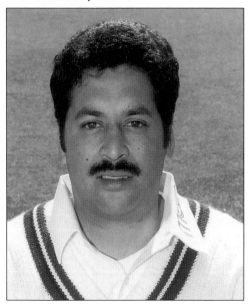

Born: Cape Town, South Africa, 19 October 1960						
Batting career:						
M	I	NO	Runs	Av	50	
233	364	22	9476	27.70	46	
253	*226*	*25*	*4616*	*20.88*	*18*	
100	**Ct/St**					
10	205					
1	*68*					
Bowling career:						
O	M	R	W	Av	5wl	10wM
748.1	151	2480	55	45.09	-	-
143	*11*	*628*	*24*	*26.16*	*-*	*-*

Career best performances:

237 v. Oxford University, Oxford, 1991

103 v. Surrey, Worcester, 1985

4-68 v. Oxford University, Worcester, 1994

3-12 v. Scotland, Glasgow

Damian D'Oliveira made his first-class debut for Worcestershire against the Zimbabwe tourists at New Road in 1982 and he played a further three matches that season, including his County Championship debut at Ilford in June, when he was leg-before to Graham Gooch for 10. During that season he played in the Birmingham League for Worcester City alongside Doug Slade and John Elliott, and in 1983 he had the City's best ever bowling figures of 8 for 47 at Gorway against Walsall.

At New Road in 1983, he scored the first of his 10 centuries with 102 in the second innings against Middlesex including 11 fours. He joined Dipak Patel after Worcestershire had lost their first three wickets for eight runs and they added 180 for the fourth wicket. At the end of this season he had scored 972 runs at 26.27, with 5 fifties to add to his maiden century.

In the winter of 1984/85, D'Oliveira went to Zimbabwe with an English Counties side led by Mark Nicholas. He played the only first-class match away from his Worcestershire appearances, scoring 22 and 6 against a Zimbabwean side at Harare that included Graeme Hick, who scored 14 and 23.

D'Oliveira reached 1,000 runs in a season for the first time in 1985 and he achieved this target three more times, with his best aggregate of 1,263 in 1990. He began opening the batting with Tim Curtis in mid-June 1985 and at Taunton they shared an opening partnership of 197, D'Oliveira's share being 113, containing 2 sixes and 17 fours, his second century of the season (this is still the best for the Worcestershire first wicket against Somerset).

There are three more Worcestershire best partnerships in the record books that include D'Oliveira, two recorded in 1990 and one in 1991. At Abergavenny in 1990 he added 264 with Hick for the third wicket, the county's best against Glamorgan, having earlier in the season shared 226 runs with Steve Rhodes, the best Worcestershire sixth wicket stand against Lancashire.

The one with David Leatherdale in The Parks is the 1991 partnership still in the record books, most of it achieved during D'Oliveira's career best 237. They added a Worcestershire best for the fifth wicket against the University – 243, with D'Oliveira hitting 7 sixes and 31 fours in 217 minutes.

D'Oliveira retired at the end of the 1994 season to become David Houghton's assistant on the coaching staff and also captain of the Second XI, although injuries caused him to be recalled for two games in 1995. When Bill Athey took over from Houghton in 1998, D'Oliveira continued in his role as assistant.

Duncan Fearnley

LHB, 1962-68

Born: Pudsey, Yorkshire, 12 April 1940

Batting career:

M	I	NO	Runs	Av	50
97	174	14	3294	20.58	14
2	*2*	*0*	*7*	*3.50*	-

100	Ct/St
1	28
-	*2*

Bowling career:

O	M	R	W	5wl	10wM
6	0	37	1	-	-

Career best performances:

112 v. Derbyshire, Kidderminster, 1966

7 v. Durham, Ropery Lane, Chester-le-Street, 1968

1-37 v. Northamptonshire, Northampton, 1968

Duncan Fearnley played two Second XI games for Worcestershire in 1960, having previously appeared for Yorkshire in the Minor Counties. The first game was at Halesowen, where he shared an opening partnership of 83 with Ron Headley before being run out for 22 and in the second innings he was bowled by Paul Munden for 11. The following season he played in all the Second XI Championship matches, finishing with an aggregate of 1,009 runs at an average of 37.37 including the first of his 10 centuries, a Worcestershire record in that competition.

Fearnley made his first-class debut in 1962 against Glamorgan at New Road, replacing Tom Graveney, and was caught by Peter Walker off Don Shepherd for 11 in the first innings. He made eight more appearances that season. When the Championship was won in 1964, Fearnley played in twenty of the twenty-eight matches with a best of 83 not out at Grace Road. Appearances became more infrequent with the qualification of Basil D'Oliveira in 1965 but, in 1966, in the middle of a run of five Championship matches, he scored his one and only first-class hundred. Derbyshire were the visitors to Kidderminster and Fearnley hit 112. It was over an hour before he got off the mark, opening with Martin Horton, and his hundred took five-and-a-half hours.

Fearnley left the staff at the end of the 1968 season but returned to captain the Second XI in 1972. During these missing seasons he played Minor Counties cricket for Lincolnshire, sharing an opening partnership of 185 in 1970 with Geoff Robinson against Suffolk at Bury St Edmunds, a Lincolnshire first wicket record at the time. A Lincolnshire record they still hold is for their first wicket in the Gillette/NatWest Trophy when they added 176 against Northumberland at Jesmond in 1971. By then Fearnley had a small corner of Fred Poole's fishing tackle shop and had begun his bat-making business, a trade he learnt in Bradford when he left school. In 1970 the now famous logo of the set of bails and stumps was being used and all types of cricket equipment were being marketed.

Fearnley handed over the Second XI captaincy to Norman Whiting in 1974, having scored a Worcestershire record 6,145 runs in the Second XI Championship. He joined the Worcestershire committee in 1977 and became its chairman in 1986, a post he held during the successful years of two Championships, two Sunday Leagues and the 1991 and 1994 Lord's finals.

Jack Flavell
LHB & RFM, 1949-67

Born: Wall Heath, Staffordshire, 15 May 1929					
Batting career:					
M	I	NO	Runs	Av	50
392	444	138	1984	6.48	1
11	*8*	*3*	*18*	*3.60*	*-*
100	**Ct/St**				
-	128				
-	*3*				

Bowling career:						
O	M	R	W	Av	5wI	10wM
11262.2	2507	32120	1507	21.31	86	15
130.2	*30*	*322*	*33*	*9.75*	*-*	*-*

Career best performances:

54 v. Warwickshire, Dudley, 1959
9 v. Sussex, Worcester, 1963
9-30 v. Kent, Dover, 1955
6-14 v. Lancashire, Worcester, 1963

Jack Flavell had played little cricket until he joined the county a week after he left the Royal Artillery at the age of twenty in 1949. Appearances with Himley and Stourbridge, where Bill Andrews was the professional, alerted Warwickshire and he was offered terms there after taking nine wickets in a Second XI match. However, Flavell thought there would be more opportunities at New Road and his Worcestershire debut came at the latter end of the 1949 season at Southend against Essex. He bowled 7 wicket-less overs for 39 runs and was bowled by Trevor Bailey for 6. This was his only appearance that season. He joined the staff the following season and had James Langridge leg before at Hove for his first wicket, finishing the summer with 20 wickets at an expensive average of 43.65. At that time he was a full-back on the West Bromwich Albion staff, but never progressed past the Central League side and joined Walsall after the 1953 cricket season was over. By then he had taken 135 wickets with a best of 6 for 43 at Kidderminster against Nottinghamshire in 1953 and had performed two of his three hat-tricks. His first hat-trick was at the expense of Kent and again at Kidderminster in 1951 where he had Arthur Phebey caught behind by Hugo Yarnold, bowled

Peter Hearn and had an eighteen-year-old Colin Cowdrey caught by Eddie Cooper. In 1953, against Cambridge University at Fenner's, his second hat-trick comprised David Dickinson, John Asquith and Richard Arkell and finished off the University innings, Flavell having taken four wickets in eight deliveries.

Flavell had one season in the Football League for Walsall, making his debut in the Third Division (South) at the County Ground, Swindon, at right-back. Twenty-one League games followed, mostly as a full-back, although he was used as a centre forward on two occasions, once in the third round of the FA Cup at Lincoln. He bowed out of League soccer and began taking more wickets for Worcestershire, getting increasingly accurate.

At The Crabble, Dover in 1955, he had figures of 9 for 30 against Kent, the second-best bowling performance for Worcestershire after Fred Root's 9 for 23 against Lancashire in 1931.

Going into the last match of the 1957 season at Blackpool against Lancashire, Flavell needed three wickets for his hundred for the season, and finished with 4 for 79 including Jackie Bond, his one hundredth wicket.

He reached 100 wickets in a season on six more occasions, with 1961 the best of them, taking 158 for Worcestershire and 171 in all matches at 17.79, an average that put him at the

Jack Flavell tees off, watched by Worcestershire colleagues.

top of the national ratings. His performances during this season earned him his Test debut against the Australians at Old Trafford, where he bowled Peter Burge for the first of his 7 wickets in a 4 Test career.

The third of Flavell's hat-tricks was a rare all leg before affair in 1963, the decisions given by umpire Fred Gardner, when Harry Pilling, Jack Dyson and Peter Lever were dismissed with successive balls at Old Trafford.

When Worcestershire won their first County Championship title in 1964, Flavell and his new ball partner, Len Coldwell, were prominent in their success. Flavell took 101 wickets in the championship at 15.08, including 9 for 56 at Kidderminster against Middlesex and 11 for 83 in the match. This ended an incredible run of four consecutive match performances. At Leyton he had match figures of 9 for 133, at Trent Bridge 9 for 100, at Cheltenham 10 for 110 – followed by his match-winning efforts at Kidderminster. Worcestershire won the title at New Road in the next match when they beat Gloucestershire and he had modest match returns of 7 for 113. In the spring of 1965 the exploits of Flavell were recognised by *Wisden*

when he was selected as one of their five 'Cricketers of the Year'.

Worcestershire retained the title in 1965 and again Flavell was instrumental in their success, with 132 championship wickets at an average of 14.99. At New Road at the beginning of August, he took 10 for 81 against Hampshire in a drawn match. In the next seven matches, all won to secure the title, he took 41 wickets including his best match figures of 13 for 96 at Kidderminster against Somerset. In the all-important last match of the season at Hove, Flavell took 7 for 26 in the Sussex first innings total of 72, a performance that put Worcestershire on the way to a 4 wickets win. Two more good seasons, with 135 wickets in 1966 and 68 in 1967, helped his career wickets tally in all matches to 1,529 and he retired at the end of the 1967 season.

His benefit in 1955 raised £6,480 and this helped him and his wife, Marie, to open 'The Rafters', a restaurant at Heathton, near Claverley; they later moved to a hotel on the west coast of Wales.

Golf was Flavell's passion during his retirement and he served the Enville Golf Club in the capacity of captain.

Geoffrey Foster

RHB, 1903-14

| Born: | Malvern, 16 October 1884 |
| Died: | Westminster, London, 11 August 1971 |

Batting career:

M	I	NO	Runs	Av	50
81	144	13	4114	31.40	19

100	Ct/St
7	89/1

Bowling career:

O	M	R	W	Av	5wl	10wM
10.3	2	48	2	24.00	-	-

Career best performances:

175 v. Leicestershire, Worcester, 1913
2-21 v. Warwickshire, Worcester, 1908

Geoffrey Foster was the fifth of the Worcestershire brotherhood of Fosters and made his debut, whilst still a Malvern schoolboy, in 1903 against Leicestershire. However, he failed to get off the mark before he was one of George Gill's five wickets. At New Road in 1905, he scored his first Worcestershire hundred with 152 against Hampshire, sharing a partnership of 181 with William Burns – still the best for the seventh wicket for Worcestershire against Hampshire.

Whilst at Oxford he won his blue in each of his four seasons, representing the university at soccer, golf and racquets, and won an amateur international soccer cap in 1907 against Holland followed by another one against Wales in 1912. His batting was below expectations for Oxford until he topped their averages in 1907 and scored a career best, at the time, of 163 against the MCC. At the end of this season he was sixth in the national batting averages, having scored 1,182 runs at an average of 40.75 in all matches. Foster scored over 1,000 runs again in 1908, his last season at university, but went to India early in 1909 to be secretary to Ranjitsinhji and

missed the whole of the cricket season. When he returned in 1910, he appeared 15 times, beat his 1908 aggregate by three runs, and added two more centuries, 123 at Stourbridge against Surrey and 129* at New Road against Sussex.

Two more centuries were added in 1913, his career best 175 in two hours and twenty minutes against Leicestershire at New Road. Later in that month of August he scored 132 at Lord's against Middlesex, where he shared a partnership of 254 with Frank Chester for the fourth wicket.

Just seven appearances in 1914 brought his Worcestershire career to an end and he moved to Kent, for whom he played ten matches, eight in 1921 and two in 1922, but with little success.

Foster was a successful businessman in financial advertising and was also secretary of the Corinthians from the end of the war until they merged with the Casuals in 1938. Peter, his son, made his debut for Kent in 1939, played one season either side of the Second World War and was elected president of the club for 1991-92. His daughter married Gerry Chalk, the Kent captain in 1938 and 1939, who was reported missing over the English Channel in February 1943 and 'presumed killed' in January 1944.

Henry 'Harry' Foster MBE

RHB & RFM, 1899-1925

Born: Malvern, 30 October 1873
Died: Kingsthorne, Hereford, 23 June 1950

Batting career:

M	I	NO	Runs	Av	50
246	441	15	15053	35.33	79
100	**Ct/St**				
28	171				

Bowling career:

O	M	R	W	Av	5wl	10wM
105.4	20	349	11	31.72	-	-

Career best performances:

216 v. Somerset, Worcester, 1903
2-16 v. Derbyshire, Worcester, 1899

Harry Foster first played for Worcestershire in 1890 and was appointed captain when they entered the Minor Counties Championship in 1895, a competition they won outright under his leadership in 1896, 1897 and 1898. When Worcestershire were elevated to the County Championship in 1899 he continued as captain, except for 1901 when his brother 'Tip' took over, and carried on up to and including 1910, before returning for the 1913 season. Foster had made his first-class debut for Oxford University, winning his blue in 1894 and again in the following two seasons. In the Varsity match of 1895 at Lord's, he scored 121, his maiden century, and the only one in his career not for Worcestershire. He also won his blue for racquets and won the amateur singles title every year from 1894 until 1900, and again in 1904.

His first century for Worcestershire was at New Road against Derbyshire, where he scored 162 in 165 minutes, hitting 20 fours and sharing a partnership of 207 with Granville Bromley-Martin, still the fourth wicket record for Worcestershire against Derbyshire. Two of his 28 hundreds for the county were turned into doubles, both at New Road, the first in 1903, his career best 216, against Somerset and the second in 1908 with 215 against Warwickshire. He reached 1,000 runs in a season on seven occasions with his best aggregate of 1,596 in 1903, the season that Worcestershire finished sixth in the Championship, their best position until he led them to the position of joint runners-up, with Yorkshire, to Nottinghamshire in 1907.

The Worcestershire first wicket record has still got Foster's name on it, since he opened with Fred Bowley against Derbyshire at Derby in 1901. They added 309 in three hours and ten minutes, with Foster scoring 152 and Bowley 140, and they were both out in the same over.

Test honours never came Foster's way and his only representative appearances were for the Gentlemen against the Players, making eight appearances in this fixture.

Foster was one of *Wisden's* five Cricketers of the Year in the 1911 edition and the following year was a Test selector for the Triangular Series between England, Australia and South Africa. He performed this role again in 1921 for the visit of Warwick Armstrong's Australians.

On leaving cricket he became a land agent in Hereford and he was awarded the MBE for his services to agriculture in the First World War. His son, Neville, played eight times for Worcestershire between 1914 and 1923.

45

Maurice Foster
RHB & RMF, 1908-34

Born: Malvern, 1 January 1889
Died: Lichfield, Staffordshire, 3 December 1940

Batting career:

M	I	NO	Runs	Av	50
157	276	8	7876	29.38	39

100	Ct/St
12	132/3

Bowling career:

O	M	R	W	Av	5wI	10wM
54.4	5	273	3	91.00	-	-

Career best performances:

158 v. Derbyshire, Worcester, 1914
2-17 v. Surrey, Worcester, 1909

Maurice Foster, the sixth of the seven Foster brothers, made his debut for Worcestershire at New Road against Lancashire in 1908 when he scored 20, the best of his three innings that season. The following season he appeared in 10 matches, scoring two half-centuries, the best of them 67 at Stourbridge, once again against Lancashire. He also had a fine season in 1909 with West Bromwich Dartmouth in the Birmingham League, the highlight of which was his 132, the highest innings for them at the time, out of a total of 272 for 5 against Stourbridge. In the autumn of that year he went out to Malaya as a rubber planter, returning in 1914 for 19 of Worcestershire's 22 matches, having an aggregate of 1,103 runs at 31.51 with two centuries. His career best was against Derbyshire at New Road in the last match before the start of the Great War, when he scored 158 in an hour and fifty minutes, hitting a six and 20 fours. Despite top scoring again in the second innings with 67, a not-out innings of 119 by

Sam Cadman saw the visitors home by five wickets.

During the war Foster went back to Malaya and played one first-class match in India for the Bengal Governers XI in the 1917/18 season, scoring 0 and 14. Bouts of malaria caused him to return home, where he joined the wine trade and played a little cricket for Worcestershire between 1920 and 1922. He was asked to captain the county in 1923, an unenviable honour with the cricketers at his disposal, Fred Root, Leonard Crawley and Vic Fox apart. He struggled on with the captaincy until the end of the 1925 season, a season when Worcestershire used forty-four players, thirty-three of them amateurs and several of them of poor quality. His last two innings of the 1926 season were 141 and 106 at New Road against Hampshire, equalling the performance by his older brothers, R.E. and W.L., against the same county in 1899. They were to be his last centuries for Worcestershire and that season saw the end of his regular cricket.

Foster joined Birmingham League club Walsall in 1932 and played until the year of his death in 1940. He served in the ARP during the Second World War and on the night of a Coventry air raid he caught a chill and died at the age of fifty-one.

Reginald 'Tip' Foster
RHB & RFM, 1899-1912

Born: Malvern, 16 April 1878
Died: Kensington, London, 13 May 1914
Batting career:

M	I	NO	Runs	Av	50
80	136	9	5699	44.87	29

100	Ct/St
13	95

Bowling career:

O	M	R	W	Av	5wI	10wM
274.5	47	1005	21	47.85	-	-

Career best performances:
246* v. Kent, Worcester, 1905
3-54 v. Gloucestershire, Worcester, 1900

The third member of the Foster brotherhood, and the most brilliant of all of them, was 'Tip' Foster. After an excellent record at Malvern School, he went to Oxford and made his first-class debut for them in 1897 against Mr A.J. Webbe's XI. He won his blue that season, as he did in the following three, but finished the season with a modest 228 runs and a top score of 53, which he scored on his debut. When Worcestershire entered the County Championship in May 1899 he joined his brothers, Harry and Bill, in the side that entertained Yorkshire in the first match at New Road. Foster returned to New Road later that month with Oxford and in their second innings, when, 16 runs short of his first century, he was caught behind off Harry. In July he finally recorded his first century, in a memorable match against Hampshire, when he scored 134 in the first innings after his brother, Bill, had scored 140. In the second innings they came together when the second wicket fell at 89 and stayed until the declaration when they had shared a partnership of 219 with Bill 172* and Tip 101*. This was the first time that brothers had scored two separate hundreds in the same match, a record that remained unequalled until Ian and Greg Chappell scored centuries in each innings of the Test match against New Zealand in 1974.

Foster was appointed captain of the University in 1900 and when W.G. Grace took his London County side to Oxford, Foster was in fine form and hit 169, with 6 sixes and 10 fours, four of the sixes struck off consecutive deliveries bowled by the Doctor. This form followed him into the Varsity match at Lord's in July, when he scored 171, hitting 24 fours in a total of 503. He played for the Gentlemen against the Players at Lord's and once again entered the record books. In the first innings he scored 102* and in the second 136, the first batsman from either side to score two centuries in the same match in this series. In all matches that season he scored 1,807 runs at an average of 51.62 and when *Wisden* arrived on the bookshelves in 1901, Foster was named as one of their five Cricketer's of the Year, becoming the first Worcestershire cricketer to receive one of these awards.

Harry was unable to play all the season for Worcestershire in 1901 so Tip took over. He played more cricket that season than any other, missing just one match, and his aggregate of 1,998 runs was a Worcestershire record until three batsman, 'Doc' Gibbons, Maurice Nichol and Cyril Walters, all had aggregates over 2,000 in 1933. In all first-class matches he scored 2,128 with 5 centuries for Worcestershire and 104* against Yorkshire in the Scarborough Festival.

The return of his brother in 1902 saw Tip spend more time away from cricket,

stockbroking. He appeared eight times for Worcestershire and in two matches at the Scarborough Festival; in 1903 he played just three matches for Worcestershire, scoring 90.

In September, Foster set sail with his wife, Clara, to Australia with P.F. Warner's 1903/04 MCC party, having turned down the invitation to tour with Archie McLaren's side two winters earlier. His early form was below average in matches before the First Test at Sydney. Australia won the toss and batted and in the second over of the match Foster's Worcestershire colleague, Ted Arnold, who was also making his debut, took the wicket of Victor Trumper, caught by Foster at slip, with his first delivery. Greater things were to follow when England replied to Australia's 285. Foster came in with the score at 73 for 3 and was last out for 287, the highest score in Test cricket until the England visit to the West Indies in 1929/30 when Andy Sandham scored 325. He was in for seven hours and shared partnerships of 192 with Len Braund for the fifth wicket, 115 with another debutant, Albert Relf, for the ninth and 130 with Wilfred Rhodes for the last wicket, which is still the best in Test cricket for this wicket. Foster played in just one first-class match in 1904 when he appeared for 'Plum' Warner's MCC Australian team against the Rest of England at Lord's in May, scoring 18 and 11; but

he returned in 1905 for seven matches for Worcestershire. In the first of these he hit a career best, and at the time a Worcestershire best, of 246* against Kent. He was 47* at close of play on the first day, was still there at lunch with 181 and when the declaration came at 627 for 9 he had batted for over four and a half hours and hit 2 sixes and 34 fours. Foster played only two games for the county in 1906 but the need for regular cricket never seemed to bother him. In the second of these matches he scored 198 out of 406 at Taunton in a high-scoring draw, appeared twelve times in 1907, scoring 3 fifties and 2 centuries and captained England in a one won, two drawn Test series against South Africa. In his next match for Worcestershire in 1910, 61 matches and almost three years later, he scored 133 against Yorkshire at New Road.

Foster was just as good an all-round sportsman as his brothers, even better when one thinks of his soccer exploits. He won a blue for soccer, and for golf and racquets, and during his time at Oxford made his soccer debut for England at Cardiff against Wales. As a Corinthian the following season he received three more caps. He is surely is the only person who will ever have had the honour of captaining his country at soccer and cricket at the highest level.

Illness, in the form of diabetes, plagued his life and he died aged just thirty-six.

Born: Middlesbrough, Yorkshire, 8 January 1898
Died: Withington, Manchester, 17 February 1949

Batting career:

M	I	NO	Runs	Av	50
163	281	31	6654	26.61	26

100	Ct/St
11	88

Bowling career:

O	M	R	W	Av	5wl	10wM
34.5	6	137	2	68.50	-	-

Career best performances:

198 v. Warwickshire, 1929
1-13 v. Yorkshire, Bradford, 1926

Vic Fox made his debut for Worcestershire at Southampton in 1923, at the time that Fred Bowley, aged forty-nine, played his last match and finished the season with 982 runs, the highest aggregate by a Worcestershire batsman during a first season. At New Road in August, Fox joined Leonard Crawley at 34 for 2 and just over three hours later they had added 306 for the third wicket, a Worcestershire record at the time and still the best for this wicket against Northamptonshire. Fox was 178 when the Worcestershire innings ended at 450 all out. Lord Harris, the great custodian of cricket's laws and morals, disputed the registration of Crawley and Fox in a well-documented argument in the Long Room at Lord's and Fox was kept out of county cricket until 1926, but Crawley then made a career with Essex and also won the English Amateur Golf Championship in 1931. Whilst Fox was qualifying he was the professional with Dudley in the Birmingham League, scoring 744 runs for them in 1925.

Before joining Worcestershire Fox was also a Middlesbrough full-back but joined Wolverhampton Wanderers in March 1925 and made his debut at Molineux against Leicester City in the Second Division of the Football League. After making 44 League appearances and 5 in the FA Cup, he moved to Newport County.

Fox returned to first-class cricket at Old Trafford in the first match of the 1926 season, scoring 44 against Lancashire before being bowled by Cec Parkin in a match plagued by the Manchester rain. He finished the season with another 3 centuries and 1,020 runs but the following season was unfortunate in his last innings to be dismissed by Charlie Parker when he was one run short of a thousand for the season. His best season was 1929, when he scored 1,457 runs at average of 31.00, with a career best 198 at Edgbaston. During this innings he hit 22 fours and shared a partnership of 141 with Percy Tarbox, still the Worcestershire ninth wicket record against Warwickshire. Fox missed only one match in 1930 but was less prolific, with 766 runs, and he left the staff at the end of the season. Poor Worcestershire batting performances in 1932 saw Fox recalled for four matches but with little success and Fox's New Road career was over.

Fox died in Withington, Manchester, following an operation, on 17 February 1949, aged just fifty-one.

George Gaukrodger

RHB & WK, 1900-10

Born: Leeds, Yorkshire, 11 September 1877
Died: Bradford, Yorkshire, 13 December 1937

Batting career:

M	I	NO	Runs	Av	50
114	177	45	2230	16.89	7

100	Ct/St				
-	169/60				

Career best performances:

91 v. Lancashire, Liverpool, 1903

When George Gaukrodger joined Worcestershire in 1900, Tom Straw was the regular wicketkeeper and during his first qualifying season he appeared in three non-Championship matches, making his debut at New Road against W.G. Grace's London County. This was Grace's only first-class match at New Road and he had match figures of 9 for 157 but Gaukrodger wasn't among his victims. He was bowled by Syd Santall in the first innings for 7, was 6* in the second and completed his first stumping when he dismissed Lionel Wells off Dick Pearson. Gaukrodger finally made his County Championship debut in 1902 at The Oval and had his best season with the bat scoring 655 runs at an average of 21.83. His first fifty came against the Australian tourists – with Dick Burrows he had a partnership of 61, the best for the Worcestershire last wicket against the Australians, and was last out when he was caught by Reg Duff off Albert Hopkins for 59. In the match at Taunton he took seven Somerset dismissals, five in the first and two in the second – a Worcestershire record

until Ernest Bale took eight in 1913 at Cheltenham, but one he equalled himself in 1907 and 1908. In the first innings at Taunton, four of his five were stumpings, three off lob bowler George Simpson-Hayward and one off Albert Bird, the most stumpings in an innings for Worcestershire, equalled by Ernie Bale in 1910 against Surrey at Stourbridge and again by Hugo Yarnold at Kidderminster against Somerset in 1949.

Later in 1902, he hit 76 at the United Services Ground, Portsmouth against Hampshire, helping to put Worcestershire in a match-winning position with a 100 runs first innings lead. Gaukrodger shared a fifth wicket partnership of 167 with Harry Foster at Liverpool in 1903, still the best for this wicket for Worcestershire in matches against Lancashire. At close of play on the first day they had added 121 and the partnership ended when Gaukrodger had reached a career best 91 on the following morning.

Prior to joining Worcestershire, Gaukrodger somehow gained a soccer international cap for Ireland at Belfast against Wales in March 1895 and scored their first goal, from the inside-left position, in a 2-2 draw. In early publications by the Association of Cricket Statisticians this Irish appearance may well have misled them to accept his birthplace as Belfast, an error corrected after research by Darren Senior.

Harry 'Doc' Gibbons
RHB & RM, 1927-46

Born: Devonport, Devon, 8 October 1904
Died: Worcester, 16 February 1973

Batting career:

M	I	NO	Runs	Av	50
380	666	57	20918	34.34	109

100	Ct/St
44	156

Bowling career:

O	M	R	W	Av	5wI	10wM
179.1	20	737	7	105.28	-	-

Career best performances:

212* v. Northamptonshire, Dudley 1939
2-27 v. New Zealanders, Worcester 1927

Harry 'Doc' Gibbons joined Worcestershire in 1927, after a spell on the ground staff at Lord's. The opportunity of a first team place with Middlesex had never materialized and he began his qualifying period for Worcestershire as professional with Dudley in the Birmingham League in 1926. It is said that his nickname was earned when he arrived at New Road at the start of his career carrying his entire cricket attire in a small leather doctor's bag. He made his debut against the New Zealanders in 1927, scoring 19 and 17, and his first season ended with a modest aggregate of 397 runs at an average of 18.04. The following season he reached the first of his twelve 1,000 runs in a season performances, and scored his first century in a splendid fashion.

Against Kent at New Road he was 0* overnight and the following morning completed his century out of 129 in 75 minutes and was bowled by Bernard Howlett for 140 before lunch. The next day at Southampton he opened the innings for Worcestershire and once more reached his century before lunch, the only batsman ever to score his first two centuries on consecutive days, both before lunch. He hit 107 in two hours before he was dismissed by Alex Kennedy with the total at 154. The West Indies tourists came to New Road in July 1928 and Gibbons celebrated with his first double century, exactly 200*, sharing a second-wicket partnership of 207 with debutant Maurice Nichol. These performances brought him to the notice of the selectors and he was chosen for the Players against the Gentlemen at The Oval, scored 84 out of 250 for 3 in his only innings in a rain-affected match. He made a second appearance in the same fixture at Bournemouth in September , this time scoring 1 and 16 for the Players and he opened the batting for the North against the South. These were the only first-class matches in his career other than those with Worcestershire.

Gibbons was a very reliable batting partner, sharing no fewer than nine partnerships of 250 or more. Two of these remained Worcestershire records until the one for the second wicket was beaten by Tim Curtis and Graeme Hick in 1986 at Neath and for the fourth, by Alan Ormrod and Younis Ahmed, in 1979 at Trent Bridge. In July 1933 at New Road, Worcestershire went in to the match with Kent with only one win to their credit that season and but for rain would have made it two. After Cyril Walters was caught by Percy Chapman off Bill Ashdown, the Nawab of Pataudi joined Gibbons and over four and a half hours later they shared

Worcestershire moved to Kidderminster to receive Warwickshire, who batted first and totalled 209. A steady reply followed until Danny Mayer took the last five wickets for seven runs leaving Gibbons to carry his bat for 70. When Worcestershire batted for a second time they required 385 to win. Walters was first out at 210 and Gibbons, having hit 13 fours, was bowled by Mayer for 100 fifteen minutes later; the spoils were shared at 282 for 3. Down the road to Stourbridge was the next place for the Gibbons bandwagon to roll with the visit of Northamptonshire. His fourth century, 129, followed during a third wicket partnership of 279 runs with Sid Martin, hitting 13 fours in 290 minutes and becoming the first Worcestershire batsman to score 4 centuries in four successive matches. Glenn Turner repeated this in 1979 and Hick in 1988, although the latter improved on this with four in consecutive innings in 1998. It is not surprising that at the end of this season he had achieved the highest aggregate for a Worcestershire batsman, with 2,654 runs at an average of 52.03, the most by anyone that season, including Don Bradman who had scored 206 at New Road during the Australian tourists' opening match. Gibbons with 0 and 1 was yet to find his feet!

Gibbons seemed to have his best seasons when the Australians were touring this country, although not against them. In six innings, one not out, he scored just 92 runs. The Australians were in Britain in 1938 and Gibbons reached the 2,000 milestone again and completed 6 centuries, the best of them against Surrey at The Oval. During a seventh wicket partnership of 197 with Dick Howorth, he scored 178 in 285 minutes, the best for this wicket by Worcestershire against Surrey. During the last season before the Second World War he hit his career best 212* at Dudley against Northamptonshire and an unbeaten century in each innings of the match at New Road against Hampshire, followed by his first 'pair' in the next match at Chelmsford. After the war he made an unsuccessful three match return for Worcestershire. He later became a director of a Fleet Street advertising firm and eventually president of the West Midlands Newspapers' Association.

274 runs, with the latter scoring 124, including 7 fours, before he was caught behind by Les Ames off Brian Valentine. Pataudi went on to 224 not out and Worcestershire's total of 477 for 2 declared was the best of their nine 400 plus scores of the season. In 1934 these two batsmen equalled this second wicket partnership at New Road against Glamorgan, when Gibbons was in a rich vein of form. Glamorgan were dismissed for 235 and Gibbons opened with Cyril Walters, the first wicket falling when the latter was out for 74 at 120. Pataudi joined Gibbons and they added 274 in 210 minutes, with Gibbons scoring 157, his second successive century, hitting 15 fours in five and a half hours.

Maurice Nichol had died suddenly during the previous match at Chelmsford, and when Worcestershire replied to the Essex first innings of 469, Walters and Gibbons opened with a partnership of 279 in three hours and ten minutes. This was their second double-century stand in successive innings following a match-winning opening partnership of 215 at Northampton. After the Glamorgan visit,

Norman Gifford MBE
LHB & SLA, 1960-82

Born: Ulveston, Lancashire, 30 March 1940					
Batting career:					
M	I	NO	Runs	Av	50
528	619	189	5848	13.60	3
273	*176*	*60*	*1267*	*10.92*	*-*
100	**Ct/St**				
-	259				
-	*75*				
Bowling career:					
O	M	R	W	Av	5wl	10wM
16132.2	5585	36071	1615	22.33	76	12
2044.2	*247*	*7931*	*308*	*25.75*	*-*	*-*

Career best performances:

89 v. Oxford University, Oxford, 1963
38 v. Warwickshire, Lord's
8-28 v. Yorkshire, Bramall Lane, Sheffield, 1968
6-8 v. Minor Counties (South), High Wycombe, 1979

Norman Gifford must have wondered what kind of a career he had chosen when he made his debut for Worcestershire at Tunbridge Wells against Kent. The game began, and ended, on Wednesday 15 June 1960 with the home side winning by an innings and 101 runs. Kent batted first and Gifford had respectable figures of 4 for 63 in a total of 187, with the wickets of Arthur Phebey, Tony Catt, David Halfyard and Alan Brown. Worcestershire were all out for 25, Gifford 0*, and, following-on, 61 all out, Gifford caught by Alan Brown off Peter Shenton for 4. The game was over by 7.15 p.m. and the Kent captain, Colin Cowdrey, described the pitch as disgraceful.

By the beginning of August 1961, Gifford had taken 100 wickets and finished the season with 133, the best haul he was to have during his long career, with a best of 7 for 37 against Sussex at Hove, 10 for 65 in the match. At New Road against Surrey earlier in the season, Worcestershire had been left to get 373 to win and Gifford joined Dick Richardson with the score at 207 for 6. When Gifford was leg before to David Sydenham, only ten runs were required and a 7 wickets victory followed thanks to 165* by Richardson and the 140 minutes of support from Gifford.

Gifford took 106 wickets in 1964, helping Worcestershire to their first Championship pennant and bringing himself to the attention of the selectors. He was chosen for the Second Test match at Lord's against the Australians, the first of what were to be 15 appearances for his country, and he took 3 for 31 in the match. Although retaining his place for the next Test, he missed out on selection again until the series against Pakistan in 1971, and on tour had his best figures at this level, in Karachi in March 1973, with 5 for 55.

At Chesterfield in 1965, Gifford took the first of his 17 seven-in-an-innings performances, the last three wickets finishing the Derbyshire innings in successive deliveries. Edwin Smith was stumped by Roy Booth, Harold Rhodes bowled and Brian Jackson caught by Ron Headley for Gifford's only hat-trick and Derbyshire had lost their last seven batsmen for 8 runs and lost by an innings.

Three years later, at Bramall Lane in 1968, Gifford had career best figures of 8 for 28 in the Yorkshire first innings of 79, following with 4 for 41 in the second in a low-scoring match won by Yorkshire, the eventual County Champions, by 4 wickets. These were his best Championship figures but in 1972 at Fenner's he had figures of

7 for 49 and 7 for 27 against the University.

A total of 7 five-wickets-in-a-season performances helped Gifford to one hundred wickets in a season for the third time in 1970. He took 105 wickets at an average of 19.92 and at the end of the season Tom Graveney left for Australia and Gifford was appointed captain for 1971. Selection for two Tests against Pakistan followed, but in the second in early August he broke a thumb whilst fielding and was out for the rest of the season.

Gifford led Worcestershire to their third Championship title in 1974 and his performance in the last match of the season at Chelmsford was instrumental in their success. He won the toss and put Essex in on what became a difficult drying pitch, which he exploited magnificently by taking 7 for 15 to claim maximum bowling points. These four points were enough to overtake Hampshire when their match at Bournemouth was abandoned without a ball being bowled.

At Northampton in 1976, Gifford joined Imran Khan with the score at 184 for 8 and together they added 127, which is still the best ninth wicket partnership for Worcestershire

against Northampton. Gifford got into the batting record books in 1979 for his performance against Sussex at Hove. Worcestershire were facing defeat when he came in at the fall of the seventh wicket and he batted for 42 overs for 1* in 98 minutes to save the game.

Early in Gifford's career the first of the three one-day competitions began, with the 65 overs Gillette Cup being the first of them. Worcestershire met Sussex in the first final at Lord's and, although on the losing side, Gifford took the man of the match award for his 4 for 33 off 15 overs. He was also in the losing side in the 1966 final and led Worcestershire in the Benson & Hedges finals of 1973 and 1976 when they were beaten each time by Kent. In the Sunday League he was the first Worcestershire bowler to take 200 wickets, finishing 1982 with 202.

At the end of the 1982 season he was released and had six good seasons with Warwickshire, captaining them between 1985 and 1987. On leaving Edgbaston he became coach with Sussex and had a similar position with Durham until 2000.

Tom Graveney OBE
RHB & LB, 1961-70

Born: Riding Mill, Northumberland, 16 June 1927

Batting career:

M	I	NO	Runs	Av	50
208	347	62	13160	46.17	79
42	*40*	*6*	*1041*	*30.61*	*5*

100	Ct/St
27	146
-	*13*

Bowling career:

O	M	R	W	Av	5wl	10wM
50.3	6	182	4	45.50	-	-

Career best performances:

166 v. Essex, Worcester, 1966
93 v. Glamorgan, Neath, 1963
2-10 v. Oxford University, Oxford, 1970

Tom Graveney, although born in the North-East, moved to Gloucestershire in 1938 with his family because of his stepfather's work. He was educated at Bristol Grammar School and all sports interested him, but in July 1939 he saw Walter Hammond and Learie Constantine at Cheltenham and his 1992 biography states he was 'determined from then on that cricket would be a part of my life, if not my living'. The Second World War put that on hold and he joined the Gloucestershire Regiment in the spring of 1945, with his cricket now played in Egypt and Greece. In 1947 he appeared in a couple of Charlie Barnett's benefit matches whilst on leave and upon demobilisation he signed for Gloucestershire on 1 April 1948, making his debut in the Parks against Oxford University a month later. He opened with George Emmett but was soon back in the pavilion, dismissed by Philip Whitcombe for 0. At the end of this first season he was 27 runs short of his thousand but achieved that milestone the following season and in twenty out of the twenty-two seasons of first-class cricket he participated in.

Graveney made the first of his 79 Test appearances against the South Africans at Old Trafford in 1951 and was bowled by Athol Rowan for 15 in his only innings. When the West Indies toured in 1957, he hit what was to remain a career best 259 at Trent Bridge, sharing a second wicket partnership of 266 with Peter Richardson and one of 207 for the third with Peter May. When George Emmett retired at the end of the 1958 season, Graveney was appointed captain but after two seasons he was replaced. In the winter of 1960 Graveney gave this statement to the press: 'On November 18 last the Club announced that one of our young amateurs, Tom Pugh, had been appointed captain. No mention of me was made in the announcement and I was neither consulted nor officially advised of the action.'

So, after 296 matches and 19,705 runs for Gloucestershire, he left and was made to qualify for a year when he chose to move to neighbouring Worcestershire. During 1961 he played for the Second XI, for Dudley,in the Birmingham League and in two non-Championship first-class matches, scoring 152* at Fenner's against Cambridge University in one of them. So began a second career and another seven seasons of 1,000 runs, with a best of 2,375 in the successful season of 1964 and a benefit in 1969 to go with his Gloucestershire one of 1959. With Martin Horton in 1962 at New Road he shared a partnership of 314 for the third wicket.

Tom Graveney (far right) and Martin Horton, with Graeme Hick and Tom Moody after the 1997 partnership at Southampton.

This was a Worcestershire record until it was dwarfed by Tom Moody and Graeme Hick in 1997 when they had a record unbroken stand of 438 for the same wicket. Graveney hit a six and 21 fours and was 164*, his fifth of six centuries hit that season, when Don Kenyon declared at 520 for 3.

At the end of the 1964 season, Worcestershire went on a World tour, covering seven different countries with the last match in Hollywood on 3 April abandoned without a ball being bowled because of rain. On that tour they played two first-class matches in Rhodesia and in the second of them Graveney scored his 103rd century with 136*, sharing a sixth wicket partnership of 99 with Doug Slade. Graveney had scored his 100th hundred during a sixth wicket partnership of 108 with Roy Booth at New Road against Northamptonshire in 1964, setting a trend for this venue having a hundred hundreds celebrations. Since his milestone Glenn Turner (1982) and Graeme Hick (1998) have also reached their 100th hundred at New Road.

Graveney played in his 55th Test at Sydney in February 1963 and 38 matches went by before he gained selection for England again. He was recalled for the Second Test match at Lord's along with debutant Basil D'Oliveira, against the West Indies in 1966, scored 96 in the first innings and shared an unbroken fifth wicket partnership of 130 with Colin Milburn in the second. When the West Indies toured again in 1969, Graveney was in the side for the First Test at Old Trafford but on the rest day he appeared at Luton for one of his benefit matches and was never chosen for England again.

When Don Kenyon retired at the end of the 1967 season, Graveney was appointed captain and held the post for three seasons. In the winter of 1969/70 he joined Queensland as coach and made two Sheffield Shield appearances, returning for one more season before retiring. A career in broadcasting followed and in 1994 he was elected president of Worcestershire, a post he held until 1997. He is still a regular at New Road with his wife, Jackie, whom he married in 1952.

Ron Headley
LHB & LB, 1958-74

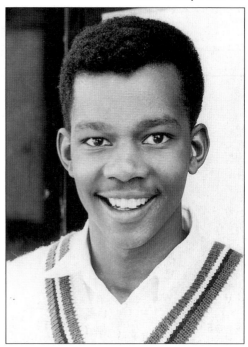

Born: Kingston, Jamaica, 29 June 1939

Batting career:

M	I	NO	Runs	Av	50
403	725	60	20712	31.14	109
120	*118*	*10*	*3445*	*31.89*	*21*

100	Ct/St
32	343
2	*41*

Bowling career:

O	M	R	W	Av	5wl	10wM
198.2	52	568	12	47.43	-	-

Career best performances:

187 v. Northamptonshire, Worcester, 1971

132 v. British Universities, Worcester, 1973

4-40 v. Glamorgan, Worcester, 1963

Ron Headley grew up in Dudley, where his father George, the great left-handed batsman, played as professional in the Birmingham League between 1951 and 1954. Ron made his first appearance for Dudley scoring 30 against Aston Unity three days before his fifteenth birthday in 1954. He made his first-class debut for Worcestershire in June 1958 against Cambridge University at New Road and in his first innings he was caught by Derbyshire opener David Green off Ted Dexter for 3. Headley became a regular in 1960 and at Romford he scored his maiden century, 108 against Essex, hitting 16 fours, and shared an opening partnership of 207 with Don Kenyon. This was to be the best of the 9 century partnerships that he shared with Kenyon. The following season, 1961, Headley completed 2,000 runs for the only time, with 4 centuries, the best of them 150* at Dudley against Somerset.

During the Championship winning years of 1964 and 1965, Headley scored 1,697 runs and 1,537 runs respectively and was the only member of the side that played in all 28 matches in each of the seasons.

When Kenyon retired at the end of the 1967 season, Headley formed a prolific opening partnership with Glenn Turner, getting Worcestershire off to some fine starts, especially in the one-day competitions.

Headley hit his career best against Northamptonshire at New Road in 1971 scoring 187, hitting a six and 23 fours, and in the second innings he became the first Worcestershire batsman since Eddie Cooper in 1946 to score 2 hundreds in the same match. His second innings score was 108 and in each innings he shared hundred partnerships with Peter Stimpson, who was making his County Championship debut, of 125 in the first and 147 in the second. During this 1971 season, Worcestershire's captain, Norman Gifford, was injured whilst playing for England and the club turned to Basil D'Oliveira and Turner to lead the side; Headley finally got the call in August. Worcestershire were then on the fringe of taking the Sunday League title, but Headley led from the front and the last three matches were won convincingly. The first was at New Road against Somerset which was won by eight runs. The next was against Lancashire at Old Trafford, the favourites to take the title; rain reduced the match to ten overs aside and Headley won the toss and batted, an unheard of decision in a 10 overs match. He opened, top scored with 36 out of 77 for 3, and then fielded

close to the bat and stopped the short singles, and a ten runs victory was orchestrated. So, the last match of the season at Dudley with Warwickshire the fodder. Warwickshire were rushed out for 126, leaving Worcestershire not only needing to win but to get the runs in 17.5 overs to get a better run-rate than Essex, who had finished their fixtures. Again, Headley led from the front with 58 and Worcestershire got home with two balls to spare. The title was not won yet however. If Lancashire could beat Glamorgan in the last match of the season at Old Trafford a week later, the title would be their's for the third season running. Clive Lloyd married his bride, Waveney, on the Saturday and perhaps the celebrations after could have had something to do with the fact that Glamorgan won by 34 runs.

Headley joined the West Indies touring party for part of the 1973 season and made his Test debut at The Oval, playing once more at Edgbaston and wearing the maroon cap with pride. The following winter he played for Jamaica, as he had done in 1965/66, and in a nine match career for them scored 489 runs at an average of 32.40, with a top score of 86 against Barbados.

Headley's last season at New Road saw him being part of the Worcestershire side that won its third Championship title in 1974. He scored 3 centuries and had an aggregate of 1,064 runs at an average of 36.68. His last match at New Road for Worcestershire was against Kent in the Sunday League and he bowed out in style, carrying his bat for 112, with 5 sixes, three in the last over off Graham Johnson, and 10 fours. Derbyshire asked him to play in one-day matches for them in 1975 and 1976 and he made a successful return to New Road in the Sunday League in 1975, scoring 87* against his old county.

Headley had gone back into the Birmingham League with Old Hill but returned to Dudley in 1981 and afterwards coached West Bromwich Dartmouth. In the 2000 season he was coach at Stourbridge.

His son Dean, who has recently retired from Kent, formerly of Middlesex, made the first of his 15 Test appearances for England in 1997.

Ted Hemsley
RHB & RM, 1964-82

Born: Norton, Stoke-on-Trent, Staffordshire, 1 September 1943

Batting career:

M	I	NO	Runs	Av	50
243	389	57	9740	29.33	53
219	*202*	*24*	*4023*	*22.60*	*17*

100	Ct/St
8	180
-	*65*

Bowling career:

O	M	R	W	Av	5wl	10wM
857.5	170	2497	70	35.67	-	-
493.3	*35*	*2201*	*73*	*30.15*	-	-

Career best performances:

176* v. Lancashire, Worcester 1977
95 Warwickshire, Worcester, 1980*
3-5 v. Warwickshire, Worcester, 1971
4-42 v. Essex, Worcester, 1971

Ted Hemsley made one appearance for Shropshire in the Minor Counties Championship and one for Worcestershire Seconds in 1961, the same year that he made his Football League debut for Shrewsbury Town at Valley Parade against Bradford City, where an Arthur Rowley goal gave them the share of the points. His successful soccer career overshadowed his cricket, with him usually arriving late in the season and leaving early. Hemsley made his first-class debut in 1963 against the touring Pakistan Eaglets at New Road, where he was run out before he had scored in the first innings. He did not feature in the 1964 or 1965 Championship winning sides, made five appearances in 1966, became a regular in 1967 and scored his maiden century, 138* in the Parks against Oxford University, in 1969.

On his return to Gay Meadow after the 1968 season, he played two games in August and was transferred to Sheffield United after 234 matches and 21 goals. He played 40 of the 42 matches when United gained promotion to the First Division as runners-up to Leicester City in 1970/71, scoring twice, one of them the only goal at Bramall Lane against Sunderland. At the end of the 1976/77 season he left United, after 247 appearances and 8 goals, and moved to Doncaster Rovers where he played out the rest

of his soccer career; his last match was at The Shay against Halifax Town in March 1979.

Hemsley was a member of the 1974 Championship winning side, but a century in that competition was still elusive and he had to wait until 1977 for his first, his previous four having been against the Universities. At New Road against Lancashire he hit a career best 176*, including a six and 22 fours, and shared a fourth wicket partnership of 213 with Glenn Turner. This was all on a pitch that the umpires reported on the first day as being unfit for first-class cricket. The following season, 1978, was his best for Worcestershire and he reached 1,000 runs for the only time. His aggregate of 1,168 included 3 centuries, the best being 141* against Leicestershire at New Road, where he shared a third wicket partnership of 211 with Alan Ormrod.

Hemsley had a benefit in 1982 and retired at the end of that season. He settled in Sheffield with his wife, Barbara, and children Steven and Jackie. For a time he was a turf accountant in Dronfield and he returns annually to New Road for the Worcestershire Old Players' reunion.

Graeme Hick
RHB & OB, 1984-present

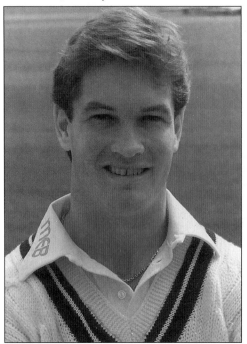

Born: Salisbury, Rhodesia, 23 May 1966					
Batting career:					
M	**I**	**NO**	**Runs**	**Av**	**50**
263	424	43	22421	58.84	82
305	*294*	*52*	*11647*	*48.12*	*79*
100	**Ct/St**				
81	322				
22	*127*				

Bowling career:						
O	**M**	**R**	**W**	**Av**	**5wl**	**10wM**
2258.2	531	6907	177	39.02	5	1
770.3	*18*	*3632*	*115*	*31.58*	*-*	*-*

Career best performances:

405* v. Somerset, Taunton, 1988

172 Devon, Worcester, 1987*

5-18 v. Leicestershire, Worcester, 1995

4-21 v. Somerset, Worcester, 1995

Graeme Hick made his first-class debut in October 1983, playing for Zimbabwe against Young West Indies at Harare against an attack that included Courtney Walsh. He arrived in England the following summer and made 964 runs at an average of 64.26 in the Worcestershire Second XI and scored four centuries, the best of them being 195 against Gloucestershire. During that season he played for Kidderminster in the Birmingham League and finished with an aggregate of 1,234 runs and a top score of 182* against Moseley, both of which were Kidderminster records and the highest innings in the league since the Second World War.

In the last match of the season at The Oval, Hick made his County Championship debut and scored 82*, sharing an unbroken partnership of 133 with Phil Neale, Worcestershire's best for the eighth wicket against Surrey. He was selected for the short Zimbabwean tour of England in 1985 and caused something of a sensation in the Parks, where he hit his maiden century and went on to score 230. In his next match, against Glamorgan at Swansea, he scored 192. During this short six-match tour he scored 598 runs and bowlers everywhere were on the lookout.

When the tour was over, Hick was off to New Road to continue his good form. He scored the first of his 81 Worcestershire centuries with 174* against Somerset, to which he added 128 against Northamptonshire and he ended the season with 1,265 runs in all first-class matches, which was clearly a superb return for a nineteen-year-old in his first full season.

Another winter followed in Zimbabwe, but this was his last season there playing cricket, for by now he had made the decision to become qualified as an England player, which he achieved by the beginning of the 1991 season. Before that, however, his batting exploits had become almost legendary. In 1986 he scored 227* at New Road against a Nottinghamshire attack that included Richard Hadlee and Clive Rice and, at the age of 20 years and 46 days, Hick was the youngest batsman to score a double century at New Road and for Worcestershire. In the following match he repeated this with 219* against Glamorgan at Neath to become the youngest batsman to score successive double centuries in the County Championship. At the end of the season he had an aggregate of 2,004 runs and, at 20 years and 111 days, he

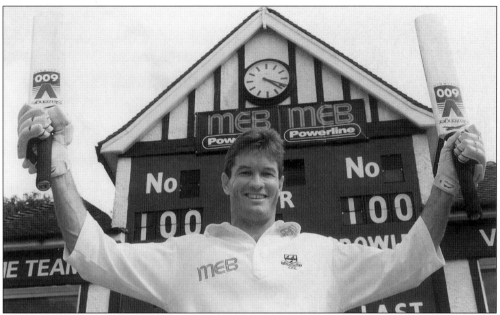

Graeme Hick celebrates his hundredth first-class century.

created another record as the youngest batsman to complete 2,000 runs in a season.

During the winters of 1987/88 and 1988/89 he played in New Zealand for Northern Districts and he is still in their record books for the highest innings, 211* against Auckland and their only batsman, with 1,228 runs, to complete 1,000 runs in a season.

In between those winters he went to Taunton in May 1988 and hit 405*, an innings that contained 11 sixes. Before the end of the month he had completed 1,000 runs, only the ninth batsman to achieve this and the first since 1973, when Glenn Turner reached this milestone. In the last match of the season he scored 197 against Glamorgan, and at ten minutes past four on the last day it was clear that Worcestershire had won the County Championship. His 1,824 the following season played a major part in the County retaining this title.

At Abergavenny in 1990, during innings of 252 and 100*, he became the youngest batsman to reach 10,000 for any county. This was the second of the four times that he has scored two centuries in the same match, one of them for Northern Districts. A winter with Queensland followed, as did three Sheffield Shield centuries

until at long last, the wait was finally over. Hick made his Test debut at Headingley against the West Indies in 1991 and by the end of the 2000 season had scored 3,257 runs at an average of 33.23 with 6 centuries in 60 Tests.

Hick scored his 100th hundred, 132 against Sussex at New Road in 1998, aged 32 years and 8 days. He was just two weeks older than the youngest batsman ever to score 100 hundreds, Walter Hammond in 1935, and is the only one to reach this target with his second hundred in the same match, having scored 104 in the first innings. His second hundred was his 73rd for Worcestershire, surpassing the previous record of 72 by Glenn Turner. Hick has been a prolific batsman in the one-day competitions, winning the man of the match award in the 1991 victory over Lancashire in the Benson & Hedges final at Lord's and in ten other matches in this competition, together with four in the NatWest Trophy. His batting record in the National League is also impressive: 7,183 runs, at an average of 45.46, and 11 centuries. In 1998 he became the seventh batsman to hit 100 sixes in the competition when he struck a delivery from Kevin Dean, dislodging a tile on the roof of the Derby pavilion.

Bunny Higgins
RHB & SLA, 1912-30

Born: Harborne, Birmingham, 31 December 1885
Died: Malvern, 3 January 1970

Batting career:

M	I	NO	Runs	Av	50
111	204	10	3837	19.77	10

100	Ct/St
3	56

Bowling career:

O	M	R	W	Av	5wl	10wM
390.4	52	1339	28	47.42	1	-

Career best performances:

123 v. Glamorgan, Kidderminster, 1927
72 v. Gloucestershire, Gloucester, 1922

John 'Bunny' Higgins made his debut for Worcestershire against Leicestershire at Stourbridgein 1912. Unfortunately rain spoiled the occasion, there being no play on the first or the third days. He was caught by Albert Lord off John King for 6 in Worcestershire's only innings, his only appearance before the First World War. After the war he played seven games when Worcestershire made their return to the County Championship in 1920. One of these matches was against Somerset at New Road, when he appeared for the first time in the same side as his brother, 'Laddie', who made 97 appearances for Worcestershire between 1920 and 1927. During the 1920s, Higgins was chief buyer for Cadbury's, and spent his winters in India. He made his first appearance for the Europeans in the 1922/23 season. Between then and the winter of 1928/29 he played ten games for them, with a best of 56 against the Parsees at Bombay in December 1923. He returned to England each summer but played just five times in 1924, twice in 1925 and not at all in 1926. During the summer of 1922 his best figures were 5 for 72 against Gloucestershire, but the match was a Worcestershire disaster. They were dismissed for 58 and 52, with Percy Mills (9 for 43) and Charlie Parker (11 for 50) bowling unchanged throughout the match, which Gloucestershire won by an innings.

His form seemed to improve on his return in 1927 and he scored 661 runs, including his first century, one of just three scored by Worcestershire batsmen that season. At Kidderminster in July he scored 123, a career best and almost half of Worcestershire's 227 all out against Glamorgan, the first Worcestershire century of the season. The end of the 1928 season saw Higgins achieve his best aggregate for a season. He reached 1,000 runs for the only time with 1,041, and added another century when he scored 101 at New Road against Yorkshire. During his last full season he scored his third and final century, 109 against Lancashire, also at New Road. His eighteen-year cricketing career ended in 1930 with just three matches that season, and he left England to spend more time in India.

During the MCC tour of India in 1933/34, there was a disagreement between the two captains, Douglas Jardine and C.K. Nayudu, on the appointment of one of the umpires, Frank Tarrant, in the Third Test Match at Madras and Higgins agreed to officiate to overcome the difficulty. Higgins was a vice-president of Worcestershire, a committee man for many years and became chairman of the cricket committee.

Vanburn Holder

RHB & RFM, 1968-80

Born: St Michael, Barbados, 8 October 1945

Batting career:

M	I	NO	Runs	Av	50
181	196	51	1553	10.71	1
163	*92*	*28*	*469*	*7.32*	*-*

100	Ct/St
-	57
-	*33*

Bowling career:

O	M	R	W	Av	5wl	10wM
5309.5	1145	13530	586	23.08	28	2
1301	*179*	*4265*	*235*	*18.14*	*-*	*-*

Career best performances:

52 v. Gloucestershire, Dudley, 1970
35 v. Middlesex, Lord's*
7-40 v. Glamorgan, Cardiff, 1974
6-33 v. Middlesex, Lord's, 1972

When Vanburn Holder joined Worcestershire in 1968 as one of their two overseas cricketers, he had already made his first-class debut for Barbados against Trinidad and Tobago at Port of Spain in February 1967, his first wicket, Inshan Ali, caught by Garry Sobers. He made his Worcestershire debut in the Parks against Oxford University in 1968 but rain ruined the match. At New Road in the next match against Gloucestershire he took his first wicket for the county, when he had Ron Nicholls caught by Worcestershire's other overseas cricketer, Glenn Turner. Fifty-nine wickets at the end of this first season at 22.01 was a good return for his initial summer in England, and this performance helped towards his selection for the West Indies touring party to England in 1969.

On this tour he made the first of his 40 Test appearances, at Old Trafford, and he bowled his Worcestershire colleague Tom Graveney for the first of his 109 wickets, his best return being 6 for 28 at Port-of-Spain against Australia in 1978. This first tour was in the early part of the season and at the end of it he returned to Worcester to complete the season and make his Sunday League debut. In this competition he became the first Worcestershire bowler to take 100 wickets, when he bowled Barry Richards at Bournemouth in 1974. This season was a memorable one for Holder, as it was his most successful with 94 wickets and a career-best 7 for 40 at Cardiff, followed by 6 for 36 against Lancashire in the next match. In the last match of the season, against Essex at Chelmsford, he took 3 for 35, which helped Norman Gifford (7 for 15) and Worcestershire to maximum bowling points and their third County Championship title.

Holder's best batting score for Worcestershire was his 52 at Dudley against Gloucestershire in 1971, when he hit 8 fours and a six out of the ground – that is sadly now a building site for a business park. In January 1974 he hit his only century for Barbados, scoring 122 against Trinidad and Tobago at Bridgetown.

On his release at the end of the 1980 season, having taken 947 first-class wickets, he had a season with Shropshire in the Minor Counties in 1981, for whom he took 76 wickets, with a best of 6 for 76 against Durham at Sunderland. During this season he was professional with West Bromwich Dartmouth, taking 58 wickets but bowling 182 no-balls. Holder is currently on the first-class umpires list, having been appointed in 1992.

Martin Horton
RHB & OB, 1952-66

Born: Worcester, 21 April 1934					
Batting career:					
M	**I**	**NO**	**Runs**	**Av**	**50**
376	665	47	17949	29.04	96
9	*9*	*1*	*278*	*34.75*	*1*
100	**Ct/St**				
22	149				
1	*3*				

Bowling career:						
O	**M**	**R**	**W**	**Av**	**5wl**	**10wM**
8277.2	2660	20381	774	26.33	38	7
56.4	*8*	*142*	*7*	*20.28*	*-*	*-*

Career best performances:

233 v. Somerset, Worcester, 1962

114 v. Hampshire, Worcester, 1966

9-56 v. South Africans, Worcester, 1955

2-20 v. Essex, Worcester, 1966

Martin Horton made his first appearance in a Worcestershire side as a fifteen-year-old in the Minor Counties Championship in 1949, but he had actually already appeared against Worcestershire in a Second XI friendly match when Northamptonshire were a player short on arrival at New Road. He came in at number ten and faced Len Blunt, who helped him off the mark. He was 2* in a total of 124 and Blunt finished with 5 for 34, 10 for 65 in the match. Three years later he made his first-class debut in the Parks against Oxford University and made his Championship debut at Old Trafford, taking the prize wicket of Cyril Washbrook, caught by Don Kenyon. National Service followed and he joined the RAF in January 1953. In the 1953 and 1954 seasons he kept company with the likes of John Murray, Peter Richardson, Fred Trueman and 'Bomber' Wells for the Combined Services and the RAF, and made occasional appearances for Worcestershire whilst on leave.

Having left the services in time for the 1954 season, he rejoined the Worcestershire staff and made an immediate impression, taking a career-best 9 for 56 in the first match of the South African tour. He bowled Worcestershire to an 117 runs win; as in 1947, they were the only county to beat them during the season. Horton ended his Worcestershire season with 1,217 runs and 95 wickets but a visit to the Torquay Festival for the North gave him the opportunity to complete his first 1,000 runs and 100 wickets double, when he took 6 for 170 in the South's first innings. In 1961 he achieved this double for Worcestershire, with 1,808 runs and 101 wickets, the last ever for the county and the first since Dick Howorth in 1947.

In a low scoring match at Bath in 1956, Horton took 6 for 38 in the Somerset first innings. In the second innings he went one better with 7 for 29, including the wickets of Harold Stephenson, Maurice Tremlett and Graham Atkinson with successive deliveries, thereby completing the hat-trick and bowling Worcestershire to a 76 runs victory. His 13 for 67 was the best of his 7 ten-wickets-in-a-match performances.

Horton scored his first double century, 212, at Leyton in 1959, sharing a partnership of 203 with George Dews, which remains a Worcestershire record for the fifth wicket against Essex. India were the touring side this

season and Horton was selected for the First and Second Tests, scoring 58 on his debut and taking 2 for 24 in the next. At the end of the season he had his best aggregate for Worcestershire, 2,123 runs at 44.22, and made his one appearance for the Players against the Gentlemen, at Scarborough. He scored 79 and shared a second-wicket partnership of 130 with a former county colleague, Peter Richardson.

During the 1962 season Horton had a share in 11 century partnerships, seven when opening with Don Kenyon. The best of them was for the third wicket, which was a Worcestershire record until it was beaten by Graeme Hick and Tom Moody at Southampton in 1997. Kenyon and Horton opened the innings at New Road against Somerset and the former was out for 97, just missing a century before lunch, when they had put on 167 in one hour and forty minutes. Ron Headley was unlucky to be out for a duck in the same over and Tom Graveney, in his first full season for Worcestershire, joined Horton. They added 314 for the third wicket, with Horton recording a career best 233, hitting 36 fours in four and three quarter hours. Worcestershire were undefeated for the first sixteen matches of this season and went on to finish runners-up to

Yorkshire, but the Championship winning side of 1964 and 1965 was coming together.

Horton played in every match during Worcestershire's 1964 County Championship winning season, scoring 1,680 runs at 31.69 and taking 46 wickets at 24.52, but missed the last run of seven consecutive victories when they retained the title in 1965. During 1966, his last season, he carried his bat for the only time in his career when he scored 53* out of a total of 91 at Old Trafford in the first innings, followed by 61 in the second to help Worcestershire to an unlikely 6-wicket win.

Horton was offered the position of New Zealand national coach and he left England in 1967. He spent three seasons playing for Northern Districts between 1967 and 1971, with a best of 109 against Wellington in January 1970 and 5 for 35 in January 1969 against Northern Districts. When he returned to England he joined the staff at Worcester Royal Grammar School and was elected to the Worcestershire committee in 1987. He became chairman of cricket in 1998 and on the death of Don Kenyon he became the president of Stourbridge Cricket Society.

Dick Howorth
LHB & SLA, 1933-51

Born: Bacup, Lancashire, 26 April 1909
Died: Worcester, 2 April 1980

Batting career:

M	I	NO	Runs	Av	50
348	571	50	10535	20.22	49

100	Ct/St
3	190

Bowling career:

O	M	R	W	Av	5wl	10wM
10840.3	2919	27218	1274	21.36	71	7

Career best performances:

114 v. Kent, Dover, 1936
7-18 v. Northamptonshire, Kettering, 1949

Lancashire-born Dick Howorth spent 1932 and 1933 qualifying for Worcestershire, playing as professional with Old Hill in the Birmingham League. During his second season there he took all 10 Smethwick wickets for 38, finishing the season with 74 wickets. He also made his first-class debut that season against the West Indian tourists at New Road, taking 4 for 102 in the match and hitting an impressive 68. His first full season was not particularly remarkable, however, as he scored just 562 runs and took 50 wickets; in the following season, 1935, he took the first of his nine 100 wickets in a season aggregates, with 125 at 19.61. In 1938 he almost completed his first 1,000 runs and 100 wickets double, missing it by just three runs. He scored 984 runs for Worcestershire and added another 13 runs for an England XI against the Australians at Blackpool at the end of the season, having already taken 108 wickets. At Kettering earlier in the season, he shared a partnership of 110 with 'Doc' Gibbons during an innings of 61, which is still a Worcestershire record for the seventh wicket against Northamptonshire.

At the end of the 1939 season, however, he did manage this double for Worcestershire in

the last match of the season. He had already completed 1,000 runs in the previous match at Dudley, against Warwickshire, and went into the last match with 94 wickets. He took three wickets in the first innings and two in the second innings, with Nottinghamshire standing at 68 for 9, but Howorth took the last wicket when he had Harold Butler caught by Charles Lyttelton. This was, in fact, the last wicket taken by a Worcestershire bowler in competitive cricket for five seasons. In the period before the Second World War, Howorth had scored 2 centuries, the first at The Crabble, Dover in 1936. He opened with Charlie Bull and they added 180 in 130 minutes, Howorth hitting 18 fours in his 114, supplementing his match figures of 8 for 91 in a Worcestershire innings win. His second was exactly 100 in 1938 at The Oval against Surrey, when he added 197 with Gibbons, a seventh wicket record for Worcestershire against Surrey.

During the war he was a professional for Walsall in the Birmingham League, scoring 687 runs and taking 60 wickets in 1940. After the hostilities, it was back to New Road for 1946 and a cold reception for the Indians. Howorth had an excellent return to first-class cricket, opening with his skipper, 'Sandy' Singleton, and scoring 105 in the second innings. He then helped to bowl the tourists to a 16 runs defeat

runs and taken 133 wickets, the only Worcestershire cricketer to complete three doubles, so it came as no surprise when he was chosen for his Test debut. When he came on to bowl he had immediate success when he had Denis Dyer caught by Cliff Gladwin off his first delivery, equalling Ted Arnold's feat back in 1903 in Australia, and had match figures of 6 for 149. Selection for the winter tour of the West Indies under 'Gubby' Allen followed and he played in all four Tests, taking 13 wickets and achieving his best figures of 6 for 124 at Bridgetown.

Howorth had 9 seven-wickets-in-an-innings performances, the best of them in 1949 when he had 7 for 18 at Kettering against Northamptonshire. His best match figures were recorded at Stourbridge in 1938 against Gloucestershire when he took 7 for 85 and 6 for 48, 12 for 133 in a match lost by 34 runs.

At Edgbaston in 1950 he took the last four Warwickshire wickets in six balls, including his only hat-trick when he had Tom Pritchard caught by Don Kenyon, Eric Hollies caught by Ronnie Bird and having Roly Thompson leg-before.

Howorth's first-class career came to an end with another hundred wickets in 1951, 124 at 18.08, and he is the only Worcestershire cricketer to accumulate 10,000 runs and 1,000 wickets. He joined Stourbridge in 1952 and took 70 wickets, and in 1954 he took 8-34 at Sandwell Park against West Bromwich Dartmouth.

He joined the Worcestershire committee in 1958 and became chairman of cricket, finding himself at the centre of a member's revolt during the 1975/76 winter. Several senior players were released and the members called for an extraordinary meeting which was to be held in the Guild Hall. As the building could not accommodate the number of members that turned up, another was arranged at Malvern Winter Gardens on 10 November. The final outcome was that Howorth resigned and in 1976 the cricket committee was chaired by Don Kenyon. Howorth invested his 1949 benefit money in a newsagents close to the County Ground, a business that was continued by his son, Brian.

with 4 for 59, having had figures of 3 for 47 in the first innings. A successful return ended with his second double, 1,050 runs and 104 wickets, once more achieving the landmark in the last match of the season by taking three Somerset wickets in the first innings and four in the second.

Howorth made an early impression on the South Africans in the opening match of the 1947 tour by taking 6 for 38 in their second innings, helping Worcestershire to a 39 runs win, making them the only county to beat them on that visit. By the time that the last Test was played at The Oval, Howorth had scored 1,170

David Humphries

LHB & WK, 1977-85

Born: Aveley, Shropshire, 6 August 1953

Batting career:

M	I	NO	Runs	Av	50
170	243	43	4969	24.84	24
157	*125*	*17*	*1551*	*14.36*	*3*

100	Ct/St
4	286/59
-	*131/35*

Career best performances:

133* v. Derbyshire, Worcester, 1984
62 v. Nottinghamshire, Dudley, 1977

David Humphries made 21 Minor Counties appearances for Shropshire between 1971 and 1973 and then spent three seasons on the staff of Leicestershire. He made his first-class debut against the Pakistanis in the first match of their 1974 tour. He was bowled by Asif Iqbal before he had scored but revenge turned out to be sweet when, in the Pakistanis' second innings, he stumped Asif off John Steele for the first of his 60 stumpings in all first-class matches.

During his time at Grace Road he was loaned out to West Bromwich Dartmouth in the Birmingham League, for whom Paddy Clift, Terry Spencer and Martin Schepens, all with Leicestershire backgrounds, often appeared. Being understudy to Roger Tolchard meant that Humphries played just once in 1975 and again in 1976 for Leicestershire. The move to New Road for the 1977 season was not opposed and he made his Worcestershire debut against Sussex. In the next match he made what was an unhappy return to Grace Road when he was caught behind by Roger Tolchard off Peter Booth before he had scored; rain then stopped play for the following two days.

The following season he scored his maiden century at New Road against Warwickshire in two and three-quarter-hours, hitting 14 fours. Lancashire were beaten by an innings at Stourport-on-Severn after Humphries and Hartley Alleyne had shared a partnership of 146, a Worcestershire seventh wicket record against Lancashire. Humphries hit 108* and took 114 deliveries to reach his century, striking 18 fours.

He scored his career best 133* at New Road in 1984 against Derbyshire when he shared an unbroken partnership of 122 with Richard Illingworth. He was in two hours and hit 4 sixes and 24 fours for his second century of the season. Earlier, at Swansea, Phil Neale declared as soon as he had reached three figures against Glamorgan after another unbroken partnership with Illingworth, this time of 138, a Worcestershire seventh wicket record against Glamorgan.

He had his best performance behind the stumps at Derby in 1979, when he took a stumping off Norman Gifford and held four catches in the first innings and three catches in the second. At the time eight dismissals in a match had only been beaten once by a Worcestershire wicketkeeper, Hugo Yarnold, with nine in 1949. When the season ended, he had an aggregate of 57 dismissals, following his 52 in 1978, and only four Worcestershire wicketkeepers have taken more in a season: Syd Buller, Yarnold, Roy Booth and Steve Rhodes.

Fred Hunt
RHB & RM, 1900-22

Born: Aldworth, Berkshire, 13 September 1875
Died: Worcester, 13 March 1967

Batting career:

M	I	NO	Runs	Av	50
53	87	18	774	11.21	-

100	Ct/St
-	17

Bowling career:

O	M	R	W	Av	5wl	10wM
447.2	77	1456	44	33.09	-	-

Career best performances:

40* v. Philadephians, Worcester, 1908
4-36 v. Essex, Leyton, 1910

Fred Hunt became a legend in his own lifetime at New Road, as their groundsman for almost fifty years. When he was appointed by the secretary, Paul Foley, in 1898, the ground was being developed and eventually staged Worcestershire's first first-class match against Yorkshire in May 1899. Prior to joining Worcestershire he had had a short career with Kent, where he had made his debut at The Mote, Maidstone in May 1897 against Gloucestershire. He scored 4 and 5, taking the wickets of Harry Wrathall and George de Winton in the first innings, but he answered Foley's call to Worcester, doubling as groundsman and medium-pace all-rounder. Hunt didn't get a game in 1899 and made his Worcestershire debut the following season against W.G. Grace's London County at New Road, the Doctor's only first-class appearance there and Hunt's only appearance of the season. He scored 7 and 2 and bowled 10 wicket-less overs.

On his return to Maidstone in 1901, Worcestershire beat Kent for the first time. Hunt had a first innings nought but in the second shared a useful partnership of 79 with Fred Wheldon for the sixth wicket, Hunt scoring 33, his best knock of the season. When Yorkshire came to New Road in 1903, Hunt bowled Billy Wilkinson and George Hirst, his first wickets for Worcestershire, finishing with 2 for 58.

Hunt's Worcestershire career may have spanned eighteen seasons, but the care of his ground took precedence over his cricket. This was shown by the fact that he made only 53 appearances over all those years, fourteen of them in 1908, the season when he had his career-best 40 not out against the visiting Philadelphians.

In Fred Root's 1937 autobiography *A Cricket Pro's Lot*, the author says ' Although it is thirty years since Hunt offered one pound each for any dandelions found within the rails, no one has yet successfully claimed the forfeit. So much for the playing field at Worcester'. In those days it flooded just once, while it sadly now sometimes floods four times during the winter months. From Root's book comes another comment: 'The flooding of the New Road enclosure is a boon, so much so that on any part of the outfield a first-class wicket could be prepared'.

Hunt farmed the land for many years on the site that, until recently, was a petrol station but is intended to be the Basil D'Oliveira Cricket School sometime in the twenty-first century.

Richard Illingworth
RHB & SLA, 1982-2000

Born: Greengates, Bradford, Yorkshire, 23 August 1963					
Batting career:					
M	I	NO	Runs	Av	50
339	387	106	6282	22.35	19
325	*157*	*74*	*1182*	*14.24*	*-*
100	**Ct/St**				
3	150				
-	*76*				
Bowling career:					
O	M	R	W	Av	5wl	10wM
9806.5	2985	23600	742	31.80	23	5
2301.2	*171*	*9070*	*351*	*25.84*	*-*	*-*

Career best performances:

120* v. Warwickshire, Worcester, 1987

36 v. Kent, Worcester, 1990*

7-50 v. Oxford University, The Parks, 1985

5-24 v. Somerset, Worcester, 1983

Richard Illingworth made one Second XI appearance for Worcestershire, at the end of the 1981 season against Nottinghamshire at Collingham, scoring 29. Match figures of 4 for 167 impressed the coach, Basil D'Oliveira, and a contract was offered for 1982. He made his debut early in the season against Somerset at New Road, where he had the wickets of Peter Roebuck, Brian Rose and Ian Botham (0) in his first spell for 61 runs. The West Indies Young Cricketers toured that season and Illingworth was selected for their English counterparts. In the first 'Test' at Northampton he had match figures of 10 for 82, and 6 for 36 in the second innings. He took the last two wickets with the last two balls of the first innings and had Phil Simmons with the first ball he bowled in the second, performing the only hat-trick at this level of youth cricket.

Illingworth joined Lawrence Smith as nightwatchman after Tim Curtis had been dismissed second ball by Allan Donald at New Road in 1987; he stayed there until the end of the innings, scoring 120*, his maiden century, off 237 balls. When he toured Zimbabwe with England 'A' in 1989/90 he scored another century as a night-watchman, 106 at Harare and another against Warwickshire with 112 in 1997. His other century for Worcestershire was a more conventional 117 against Nottinghamshire, at

Trent Bridge in 1990, batting at number seven.

At Southampton in 1997, Graeme Hick and Tom Moody shared a record unbroken fourth wicket partnership of 438, a performance that was followed by Illingworth's career-best Championship figures of 7 for 79. This performance finished with match figures of 10 for 147 in a nine-wicket win.

Illingworth made the first of his nine Test appearances against the West Indies in 1991 at Trent Bridge, where he bowled Simmons with his first delivery to equal the achievements by previous Worcestershire bowlers Ted Arnold and Dick Howorth in the past. Four years later he had his best Test figures against the same opponents and at the same venue, when he took 4 for 96. Illingworth went on three tours with England, to Pakistan, New Zealand and South Africa, and had a season in South African cricket with Natal in 1988/89.

At Hove in 1993 he completed the only hat-trick by a Worcestershire bowler in one day cricket when he dismissed Peter Moores, Tony Pigott and Ed Giddins with consecutive deliveries in the Sunday League. When he was released by Worcestershire at the end of the 2000 season, he was their leading bowler in that competition with 264 wickets. Derbyshire gave him the opportunity to continue his career and he joins them for 2001.

Imran Khan
RHB & RF, 1971-76

Born: Lahore, Pakistan, 25 November 1952

Batting career:

M	I	NO	Runs	Av	50
42	67	6	1518	24.88	6
48	*41*	*10*	*1150*	*37.90*	*11*

100	Ct/St
4	19
-	*8*

Bowling career:

O	M	R	W	Av	5wI	10wM
1095.5	203	3150	128	24.60	7	1
382.2	*31*	*1507*	*56*	*26.91*	*-*	*-*

Career best performances:

166 v. Northamptonshire, Northampton, 1976
75 v. Warwickshire, Worcester, 1976
7-53 v. Lancashire, Worcester, 1976
5-29 v. Leicestershire, Leicester, 1973

Imran Khan came to England with the 1971 Pakistani touring side, making his Test debut whilst still only an eighteen-year-old. At the end of the tour he joined Worcestershire and made his debut against the Indians at New Road, where he was run out in the first innings before he had scored. At the end of the season he went to the local Royal Grammar School where he studied for his A levels, eventually getting a place at Oxford University in 1973. He won a blue that season and in the following two, and captained the side in 1974. Worcestershire only chose him for Second XI cricket in 1972, where he played in nine games without distinguishing himself, but after leaving university in 1973 he made his County Championship debut at Edgbaston, where he took his first wickets, those of Steve Rouse and David Brown.

His last season for Worcestershire, 1976, was no doubt his best. He scored 1,092 runs and took 65 wickets, with his best performance for them being against Lancashire at New Road, where he returned an all-round performance achieved only once before by a Worcestershire cricketer. In 1909 Ted Arnold had a match double of over 100 runs and 10 wickets in the same match and on this occasion Imran scored 111* and then destroyed the Lancashire batting with 7 for 53 and 6 for 46, achieving a one-man

innings victory. Later in the season he had his best batting performance of 166 at Northampton, where he had a partnership of 127 with Norman Gifford, which is still the best for the ninth wicket for Worcestershire against Northamptonshire.

Imran left at the end of the 1976 season to join Sussex and was accused of disloyalty, but this quote from his 1983 biography denies this: 'The slurs about my disloyalty hurt me. When I joined Worcestershire in 1971, my loyalty was to the two men who had asked me there: Joe Lister and Wing Commander Shakespeare. Yet when I reported in 1972, they had gone and the new administration soon let me know that things weren't going to turn out as I expected'.

During his 88 Test appearances he scored 3,807 runs and took 362 wickets. He was the third Worcestershire cricketer, behind Kapil Dev and Ian Botham, to reach the 3,000 runs/300 wickets double, and in 1993 he led Pakistan to victory over England in the World Cup final in Melbourne. He retired to a political career in Pakistan and help with fund-raising for a hospital in memory of his mother.

John Inchmore

RHB & RFM, 1973-86

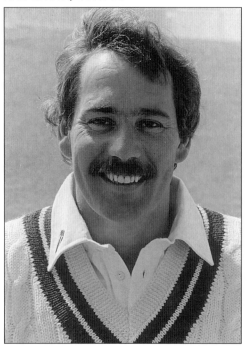

Born: Ashington, Northumberland, 22 February 1949					
Batting career:					
M	I	NO	Runs	Av	50
216	243	53	3137	16.51	7
226	*149*	*44*	*1462*	*13.92*	*-*
100	**Ct/St**				
1	72				
-	*48*				
Bowling career:					
O	M	R	W	Av	5wl	10wM
4936	965	14546	503	28.91	18	1
1764.3	*166*	*6893*	*277*	*24.88*	*-*	*-*

Career best performances:

113 v. Essex, Worcester, 1974
49* v. Somerset, Taunton, 1976
8-58 v. Yorkshire, Worcester, 1977
6-29 v. Lancashire, Old Trafford, 1984

John Inchmore moved south to Birmingham to train as a teacher at St Peter's College, Saltley and played his cricket for Stourbridge in the Birmingham League, having made three appearances for Northumberland in the Minor Counties Championship in 1970. After appearances for Worcestershire and Warwickshire Second XIs in 1972 he joined the Worcestershire staff for the following season, making his debut in the first match of the season against the touring New Zealanders, who included Glenn Turner. Turner had scored 143 when Inchmore bowled him for his first first-class wicket.

Towards the end of Worcestershire's Championship winning season of 1974, Essex were the visitors to New Road. Turner had to retire hurt shortly before close of play on the Saturday evening so Inchmore joined John Parker as night-watchman, with the score at 65 for 3. Turner was unfit to resume on the Monday so this unusual fourth-wicket pairing continued, with Inchmore reaching his one and only century with 113 in four hours, finishing with a stand of 266, a record for the fourth wicket for Worcestershire against Essex.

Another batting performance that Inchmore is well remembered for was his 64 against Yorkshire at Bradford in 1980. He hit 7 sixes, most of them over the old football stand, in 35 minutes off 26 balls in a partnership of 70 with Barry Jones, whose share in the stand was 3. Yorkshire were also on the end of Inchmore's career best when he took 8 for 58 in their first innings and 2 for 10 in the second at New Road in 1977, his only ten wickets in a match performance.

Inchmore won one man of the match award in the NatWest trophy in 1985 for his 5 for 25 performance against Glamorgan at Swansea. Rain delayed the start until six o'clock – the members of the Worcestershire Supporters Association coach had actually given up and gone to Porthcawl for the day – and Glamorgan, at the close, were in trouble at 51 for 4. The following morning Inchmore took 4 wickets to finish off the innings and Worcestershire reached the semi-final thanks to a 4-wicket win.

In the first Benson & Hedges Cup match of 1976, Inchmore won the first of his three gold awards for his 49* and 2 for 36 against Somerset at Taunton and he scored 992 runs and took 169 wickets in the Sunday League.

Towards the end of his career he joined Allied Dunbar Assurance and in 1987 he was elected to the Worcestershire committee.

Peter Jackson
RHB & OB/RM, 1929-50

Born: Aberfeldy, Perthshire, 11 May 1911
Died: Harrogate, Yorkshire, 27 April 1999

Batting career:

M	I	NO	Runs	Av	50
383	546	208	2044	6.04	-

100	Ct/St
-	194

Bowling career:

O	M	R	W	Av	5wI	10wM
11797.2	2737	30209	1139	26.52	58	11

Career best performances:

40 v. Gloucestershire, Worcester, 1933
9-45 v. Somerset, Dudley, 1931

Peter Jackson, who was actually christened Percy but answered to Peter all his cricket life, made his debut against Lancashire in 1929 at New Road, where he was dismissed for the first of his Worcestershire record 15 'pairs' and bowled 32 wicket-less overs for 120. His fortunes changed in the next match when he took 6 for 67 at Gloucester; by the end of his first season he had taken 49 wickets. In 1935 Jackson celebrated his twenty-fourth birthday in style by playing at Lord's. He took 8 Middlesex wickets for 64 on the Saturday and took another 4 on Monday for match figures of 10 for 119. Later that season he had his career-best figures in the Somerset second innings at Dudley when he took 9 for 45, having taken 4 for 68 in the first innings.

At the end of the 1936 season he had taken 112 wickets, the first of his four 100 wickets in a season performances, and at Neath he completed his only hat-trick when he dismissed Dai Davies, George Lavis and Arthur Porter with successive deliveries. He took 102 wickets the following season, but a back injury sustained in a collision with Lancashire's Eddie Phillipson at Dudley in 1938 kept him out of the game for a while and his aggregate for the season dropped to 46 wickets. During the last season before the Second World War, Jackson signed as professional for Old Hill in the Birmingham League and, apart from two matches, only appeared for Worcestershire in matches started on Wednesdays.

Jackson was regularly played for Worcestershire after the war and topped the bowling averages in 1946 with 118 wickets at an average of 19.61, taking five wickets in an innings on 10 occasions. When the Australians opened their 1948 tour at New Road, Jackson had impressive figures of 6 for 135 off 39 overs, his wickets including Don Bradman, Lindsay Hassett and Arthur Morris.

When Jackson left at the end of the 1950 season, he had scored 2,044 runs, the most by any Worcestershire batsman without ever hitting a 50. His career-best performance was at New Road in 1933 when he hit 40 and shared a ninth wicket partnership of 68 with Bernard Quaife, a stand that saved the follow-on. The best partnership he shared was one of 72 with Roly Jenkins at Chelmsford in 1947, which is still the best for the Worcestershire final wicket against Essex.

After leaving first-class cricket he went back into the Birmingham League with Old Hill.

Roly Jenkins
RHB & LB, 1938-58

Born: Worcester, 24 November 1918
Died: Worcester, 21 July 1995

Batting career:

M	I	NO	Runs	Av	50
352	530	109	9215	21.88	37

100	Ct/St
1	197

Bowling career:

O	M	R	W	Av	5wI	10wM
8618.2	1502	27240	1148	23.72	80	17

Career best performances:

109 v. Nottinghamshire, Trent Bridge, 1948
8-62 v. Sussex, Dudley, 1953

Roly Jenkins made his debut against Essex at Southend in 1938 and, while he didn't get a chance to bowl in this particular game, he took 35 wickets in the following thirteen matches he appeared in during that first season. He became a regular in the side the following year, but then lost five summers to the Second World War. On his return from serving in the Worcestershire Regiment as a physical training instructor in 1946 he re-joined the Worcestershire staff and impressed early on, taking 8 for 92 at Old Trafford. He had an aggregate of 1,097 runs in 1947 but had his best season with the bat in 1948 when he finished with 1,310, and scored his only century. At Trent Bridge he hit 109 and shared a match-saving second wicket partnership of 170 with Fred Cooper, who was also scoring his only first-class century. On the following day at The Oval he took the wickets of Bernie Constable, Eric Bedser and Stuart Surridge with successive balls, thereby completing the first of his three hat-tricks, all performed against Surrey. His other two were both performed in the same match at New Road in 1949, when he dismissed Jack Parker, Alec Bedser and Stuart Surridge in the first innings and Michael Barton, Arthur McIntyre and Alec Bedser in the second, an achievement that had only been performed in the same match three times before and once since.

In between the New Road and Oval hat-tricks, Jenkins went to South Africa with the MCC party under George Mann for the winter of 1948/49. It was a late call, replacing an injured Eric Hollies, so his marriage to Olive had to be postponed until he returned. He had a very successful tour, making his Test debut at Durban. It was there that he took his first wicket, when he had Eric Rowan caught behind by Godfrey Evans with his third ball, and finished on top of the England Test averages with 16 wickets.

He failed to get selected for any of the 1949 Tests against New Zealand, although he took 183 wickets and scored 1,183 runs overall, collecting 16 five wickets in an innings performances and 5 of ten wickets in a match. However, he did play for the Players against the Gentlemen at Lord's, taking 4 for 48 in the second innings and sharing a match-winning, unbroken seventh wicket partnership of 70 with Godfrey Evans. He shone with the bat when he joined Bob Wyatt at New Road against Leicestershire, and they shared a partnership of 190, the best for Worcestershire's seventh wicket against Leicestershire. Jenkins reached his 1,000 runs, and his double, when he had scored 29 and went on to 80, his fourth fifty of the season.

Jenkins took over 100 wickets in 1950 and he

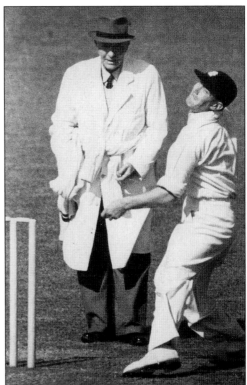

Whether practice or the real thing, Roly always bowled in a cap.

was recalled by England for the Second Test against the West Indies at Lord's. Here he took 5 for 116 and 4 for 174 in a match that saw the visitors have their first victory in England, by a massive 326 runs. He played the last of his nine Tests at Lord's against India in 1952, the season when he completed his second, and last, double in all matches with 1,087 runs and 136 wickets.

Jenkins began 1953, his benefit season, in fine form, having taken 60 wickets by the middle of June, including his career-best performance against Sussex at Dudley where he took 8 for 62 and 7 for 60, his best innings and match analysis. A knee injury in the match at Hinckley, however, kept him out of the side for the rest of the season.

The last of his 100 wickets in a season aggregates were taken in 1956 at Grace Road during the penultimate match of the season. Going into the match with 96 wickets, he had figures of 6 for 46 in the first innings and

5 for 67 in the second, his 100th victim being Jack Firth, hit wicket. In the first Championship match of that season he took 8 for 86 at Hove on the last day, when 14 wickets fell for 251 runs. Jack Flavell took the wicket of Don Smith in the first over of the second innings and Jenkins took the next eight, but Sussex won by one wicket thanks to an unbeaten 106 by Jim Parks.

Jenkins finished his cricket career at the end of the 1958 season and invested in a sweet shop in the City near the hop market. Until his retirement he worked as a foreman for Libbys. He is a cricketer who probably put more into the game when he finished playing than when he played, and he was always ready help any cricket society that had been let down at the last minute. For many years he looked after cricket at Ombersley Cricket Club, coaching, umpiring and generally helping out, and he was sadly missed by all when he died in 1995.

Maurice Jewell

RHB & SLA, 1909-33

Born: Iquique, Chile, 15 September 1885					
Died: Birdham, Sussex, 28 May 1978					
Batting career:					
M	I	NO	Runs	Av	50
121	220	13	3906	18.96	19
100	**Ct/St**				
2	62				

Bowling career:						
O	M	R	W	Av	5wl	10wM
1018.1	159	3217	98	32.82	2	-

Career best performances:

125 v. Hampshire, Worcester, 1926

7-56 v. Warwickshire, Worcester, 1919

Maurice Jewell first played for Worcestershire in 1909, against Oxford University in Worcestershire's only twelve-a-side first-class match. That was his only appearance for the county until after the First World War; he appeared in 1914 for Surrey Seconds and played in two County Championship matches for Sussex, both at Hove. The first match was against Worcestershire, when he scored 50 in an innings win, followed by 5 against Yorkshire in a drawn match. During the war he served in France as a Major, commanding a battery of the Royal Field Artillery, and in 1919 he returned to an unusual season of cricket. He played four matches for Sussex, one of them at Tonbridge on 20 and 21 June, and then appeared for Worcestershire at New Road against Gloucestershire on 23 and 24 June. He went back to play for Sussex against Cambridge University on 26 and 27 June. Worcestershire had not entered the County Championship that season and their matches were two-day, first-class friendlies, but Jewell was one of the few twentieth century cricketers to play for two counties in the same season. At New Road he had career-best figures of 7 for 56 on a drying wicket against Warwickshire. In this match his brother, Arthur, who was also in the

Worcestershire side, opened the innings with Fred Bowley.

Maurice then left Sussex and took on the captaincy of Worcestershire in 1920 and again in 1921. These were hard times for the county, which won just six of the thirty matches that were played during that period. Jewell was unable to play for much of the next four seasons and his brother-in-law, William Taylor, took over but little else changed. Worcestershire finished bottom in 1922 and two from bottom under Maurice Foster in 1923.

Jewell returned to the captaincy in 1926 and had his best season with the bat, scoring 920 runs with two centuries, both against Hampshire. The first was at Portsmouth, where he scored 103 and shared an opening partnership of 181 with Les Wright and, in the return at New Road, a career-best score of 125. During this season he also took the second of his five wickets in an innings performances, when he had 5 for 69 at Stourbridge against Leicestershire.

Jewell played relatively little cricket after 1926 and he made his last appearance in 1933, scoring 3 and 16 against the touring West Indians at New Road. He was elected president of the club in 1950 and remained in this post until 1955. In 1971 he celebrated sixty years of marriage to his wife, Elsie.

Kapil Dev
RHB & RFM, 1984-85

Born: Chandigarh, India, 6 January 1959

Batting career:

M	I	NO	Runs	Av	50
24	40	6	1456	42.82	11
26	*23*	*1*	*341*	*15.50*	*-*

100	Ct/St
1	21
-	*16*

Bowling career:

O	M	R	W	Av	5wl	10wM
601.2	158	1624	72	22.55	2	-
199.2	*19*	*802*	*26*	*30.84*	*-*	*-*

Career best performances:

100 v. Middlesex, Lord's, 1985
40 v. Sussex, Worcester, 1984
5-30 v. Somerset, Worcester, 1984
5-52 v. Lancashire, Old Trafford, 1985

Kapil Dev joined Worcestershire as their overseas player in 1984, but missed the first six weeks of the season following a knee operation. When he did arrive in June, he immediately made an impression with an innings of 95 against Hampshire at New Road, sharing a fifth wicket partnership of 153 with David Smith. He finished the season with 640 runs at an average of 42.66, with 6 fifties, and 35 wickets at 23.40, with a best score of 5 for 30 at New Road against Somerset. Worcestershire had been eliminated from the Benson & Hedges Cup before Kapil's arrival and, after beating Suffolk in the first round of the NatWest Trophy, they went to Northampton for the second round. Much was expected of Kapil, who was returning to the county he had played with for three seasons between 1981 and 1983. He bowled 12 tidy overs for 27 with one wicket, but was bowled for 2 by Neal Mallender, who won the man of the match award for his 7 for 37, the best figures in this competition against Worcestershire.

Kapil again made an early impression in 1985, when he scored 100 at Lord's in the opening match of the season. His first eight scoring shots were all fours and he hit 8 more as well as 2 sixes, one of which was off Norman Cowans, to go to his century off 78 balls in 75 minutes. Worcestershire got to the semi-final of the NatWest Trophy in 1985, but were beaten by Nottinghamshire when Kapil had returned home. In the second round at Old Trafford he had his best Worcestershire one-day figures of 5 for 52, but an innings of 91 by Clive Lloyd won the man of the match award.

At this time he was captain of India, so he was called away to lead them in Sri Lanka, missing the last nine Worcestershire matches, with Graeme Hick taking over as their overseas cricketer. India were to tour England in 1986, so Kapil's contract was not renewed.

Kapil was a great all-rounder for India, scoring 5,248 runs at 31.05 and taking 434 wickets at 29.64. One innings that stands out took place at Lord's in 1990 when India were 430 for 9, needing 24 to save the follow-on. Kapil became the first batsman in Test cricket to strike 4 successive sixes, all off Eddie Hemmmings, and England had to bat again.

When allegations were made in September 2000 that he was involved in a betting scandal in Sri Lanka in 1994, Kapil resigned as coach of India halfway through his two-year contract.

Don Kenyon

RHB, 1946-67

Born: Wordsley, Staffordshire, 15 May 1924
Died: Worcester, 12 November 1996
Batting career:

M	I	NO	Runs	Av	50
589	1060	51	34490	34.18	165
10	*10*	*0*	*118*	*11.80*	*-*

100	Ct/St
70	306
-	*1*

Bowling career:

O	M	R	W	Av	5wl	10wM
33.5	0	178	1	178.00	-	-

Career best performances:

259 v. Yorkshire, Kidderminster, 1956
42 v. Glamorgan, Newport, 1964
1-8 v. Pakistan, Worcester, 1967

Don Kenyon was noticed by Worcestershire just before the Second World War because of his exploits with Stourbridge in the Birmingham League. In August 1939 he scored 103 against Aston Unity and, at the age of 15 years and 80 days, he was the youngest batsman to reach three figures in the oldest league. He joined the RAF shortly after his eighteenth birthday, but had ample opportunity to hone his cricket skills in Cambridgeshire. He played with the RAF and the Combined Services and made his Worcestershire debut at New Road against Surrey whilst still in the RAF. On the strength of his performances he was offered a contract on demobilisation in December 1946, and played in every Championship match of the 1947 season and was awarded his county cap. Kenyon lost his place to Fred Cooper in 1948, but struck form in 1950, scoring the first of his six 2,000 runs in a season aggregates. Selection for Nigel Howard's MCC party to India, Pakistan and Ceylon followed the 1951 season and at Delhi he made the first of his 8 Test Match appearances.

Kenyon has shared a Worcestershire record of 124 century partnerships, twenty-two of them with Peter Richardson, including his best of 290 for the first wicket at Dudley in 1953 against Gloucestershire in just under five hours. In 1953 he scored the first of his seven double centuries with 238 not out against Yorkshire at New Road; but at Kidderminster three years later he scored 259 against Yorkshire, the highest innings against them in the twentieth century. He batted for seven hours and thirty-five minutes, hit 38 fours and shared partnerships of 117 for the third wicket with George Dews and 144 for the fifth with Martin Horton.

At Eastbourne in 1957, Kenyon scored 123 against Sussex, his 45th century for Worcestershire, beating the previous record of 44 by 'Doc' Gibbons. Kenyon retired with 70 Worcestershire centuries, a record that lasted until 1982, when he was overtaken by Glenn Turner, who in turn was replaced by Graeme Hick in 1998.

When Peter Richardson defected to Kent during the winter of 1958/59, Kenyon was appointed captain and the beginnings of a Championship-winning side were showing signs of developing. He led from the front from the start – with five centuries amongst 1,613 runs with a superb 229 out of 337 at Portsmouth against Hampshire in six and a half hours with 2 sixes and 33 fours, his second century on this United Services Ground. The 1950s ended with Kenyon having scored 20,087 runs in that ten year period, the most by any Worcestershire batsman in any decade up to the end of the

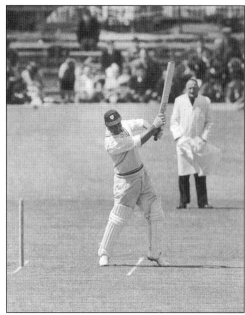

Left: Don Kenyon (left) and Surrey captain Peter May toss for the choice of innings at New Road. Right: Kenyon drives through the covers.

twentieth century. Kenyon led Worcestershire to the runners-up spot behind the champions Yorkshire in 1962, their best position since 1907; for his efforts he was chosen as one of *Wisden*'s Five Cricketers of the Year when the 1963 edition was published in the spring.

A well balanced side was slowly beginning to take shape under Kenyon and in 1964 Worcestershire won the County Championship for the first time in their history when they beat Gloucestershire at New Road with three matches to spare. Kenyon celebrated this success by scoring 158 not out in the next match against Sussex at Eastbourne. This was his third, and best, century of the season, scoring 20 fours in five and a half hours.

During the winter of 1964/65 Kenyon led Worcestershire on a seven-country, 34,000 mile world tour, playing two first-class matches in Rhodesia and ending in Hollywood, USA where it rained and the match was abandoned without a ball being bowled. The Championship was retained the following season when Worcestershire won their last seven matches, ending with the tense finish at Hove when the winning run, and the title, came with just seven minutes remaining.

Kenyon was invited to join the Test selectors in 1965, a position he held until 1972. It caused him to miss some of his Worcestershire cricket and his form suffered. During his last three seasons, 1965-67, he scored a modest 2,708 runs at an average of 23.34, including three centuries, and he played his last innings against Glamorgan at Colwyn Bay on 1 September 1967. He lost his opening partner, Ron Headley, early and was joined by Alan Ormrod. They added an unbroken 111 with Kenyon's share being 67, bringing his Worcestershire aggregate to 34,490 runs, a figure that will almost certainly never be overtaken.

Kenyon joined the Worcestershire Committee in 1968, remaining in office until 1982. At the club's AGM in March 1986 he became the first ex-professional to be elected president of Worcestershire, a post he held with much distinction until 1990.

Kenyon married Jean at St James' church, Wollaston in 1947 and they lived all their married life in Wordsley, in the heart of the Black Country.

Stuart Lampitt

RHB & RFM, 1985-present

Born: Wolverhampton, Staffordshire, 29 July 1966					
Batting career:					
M	I	NO	Runs	Av	50
225	298	69	5444	23.77	19
249	*152*	*47*	*1849*	*17.60*	*1*
100	**Ct/St**				
1	143				
-	*73*				

Bowling career:						
O	M	R	W	Av	5wl	10wM
5112.2	1068	16460	576	28.57	19	-
1670	*110*	*7387*	*305*	*24.21*	*-*	*-*

Career best performances:

122 v. Middlesex, Lord's, 1994
54 v. Scotland, Edinburgh, 1998
7-45 v. Warwickshire, Worcester, 2000
6-26 v. Derbyshire, Derby, 1994

Stuart Lampitt made his debut at Fenner's in 1985, one of six players making their first-class debuts for Worcestershire, three of whom never played at that level again. The match was ruined by rain and he had to wait over twelve months for his next appearance, against Sussex at Hove, his only appearance of the 1986 season. That 1986 season had a memorable end for Lampitt when he played for his Birmingham League club at Lord's in the William Younger Cup final against Weston-Super-Mare. He took 5 for 43 and hit 32, adding 76 for the third wicket with Harshad Patel, one of those six debutants in 1985.

Worcestershire won the Sunday League title in 1987, with Lampitt making six appearances in that competition, and taking his first wicket, Geoff Humpage, caught by Tim Curtis, at New Road. Lampitt was a valuable member of the Worcestershire County Championship-winning side in 1989, having the first of his five wickets in a single innings performances when he took 5 for 32 in the Kent second innings at New Road. Along with Steve McEwan, Lampitt received his county cap at the end of the season and he has been a regular member of the side ever since. He scored his one and only century against Middlesex at Lord's in 1994, finishing with 624 runs and a season's best tally of 64 wickets.

At Kidderminster in 1991, Worcestershire followed-on 154 runs behind Derbyshire and when Lampitt joined Steve Rhodes with the score at 163 for 7, a defeat looked the most probable result. A Worcestershire record eighth wicket partnership of 184 followed, with Rhodes scoring 90 and Lampitt 93, and the game was saved. This was one of six century partnerships that he has shared with Rhodes.

Lampitt became one of three Worcestershire cricketers to have completed the 1,000 runs/100 wickets double in the Sunday League when he reached his 1,000 runs at Northampton in 1997, following Basil D'Oliveira (1977) and Neal Radford (1995). In this competition at Northampton in 1997, Worcestershire required sixteen runs to win off the last over which was to be bowled by John Emburey, playing in his last match for Northamptonshire. Lampitt hit his first delivery for six followed by two, two, four and a two that won the game with a ball to spare.

At Derby in 1994 he won the gold award for his 6 for 26 in the Benson & Hedges Cup quarter-final and the man of the match award for his 5 for 22 against Suffolk at Bury St Edmunds in the NatWest Trophy in 1990. He was also in the side that beat Lancashire at Lord's in 1991 and Warwickshire in 1994.

David Leatherdale

RHB & RM, 1988-present

Born: Bradford, Yorkshire, 26 November 1967

Batting career:

M	I	NO	Runs	Av	50
179	289	34	8446	33.12	46
212	*176*	*28*	*2881*	*19.46*	*10*

100	Ct/St
12	138
-	*89*

Bowling career:

O	M	R	W	Av	5wI	10wM
830.5	171	2854	95	30.04	2	-
380.4	*13*	*1885*	*85*	*22.17*	*-*	*-*

Career best performances:

157 v. Somerset, Worcester, 1991

70* v. Yorkshire, Worcester, 1999

5-20 v. Gloucestershire, Worcester, 1998

4-13 v. Minor Counties, Worcester, 1997

David Leatherdale made his Worcestershire debut in 1988 at Grace Road, having played for the Second XI for the first time at Ombersley against Leicestershire in the last match of the 1985 season. In 1987 at the Imperial Ground, Bristol, he scored the first of his twelve Second XI Championship centuries with 109 against Gloucestershire, sharing a fourth-wicket partnership of 229 with Martin Weston. Although he had played only eight first-class matches he was chosen for the Worcestershire side in the NatWest final against Middlesex in 1988, having appeared in three of the early rounds. His 29 was second top score to Phil Neale's 64 at Lord's in one of those many early morning disappointing batting performances. Another young man was to take the plaudits, man of the match Mark Ramprakash, for his match-winning 56.

Leatherdale spent most of the 1991 season in the Second XI, but when given his first chance that season in the County Championship he made the best of the opportunity, scoring what is still a career best, 157 at New Road against Somerset, and sharing a third-wicket partnership of 256 with Tim Curtis. The following season he played in every match, finishing just 17 runs short of 1,000, and was not to reach this magic figure until 1998, when he scored 1,001 at an average of 33.36.

Leatherdale has been in several late order partnerships, two of them Worcestershire records against Essex and Somerset at Chelmsford and Taunton respectively. In 1993 he shared a ninth-wicket partnership of 142 with Richard Illingworth, the best for this wicket against Essex, and in 1994 added 183 with Illingworth again for the best eighth-wicket by Worcestershire against Somerset.

Leatherdale's best season was probably in 1997 when he scored 886 runs at an average of 52.11 and had his best haul of 26 wickets for the season. He scored centuries against Kent and Northamptonshire, 129 and 110 respectively, in consecutive matches and had his first five wickets in an innings performance when he took 5 for 56 at New Road against Somerset.

At New Road in 1999 he had his best one-day innings in the National League against his native Yorkshire, scoring 70 not out in a fourth-wicket partnership of 133 with Gavin Haynes and in the return match at Headingley he scored 54, his second fifty of the season.

Joe Lister

RHB, 1954-59

Born: Thirsk, Yorkshire, 14 May 1930
Died: Harrogate, Yorkshire, 28 January 1991

Batting career:

M	I	NO	Runs	Av	50
21	37	4	750	22.72	4
100	**Ct/St**				
-	11				

Career best performances:
99 v. Kent, Worcester, 1955

After three years in the Cheltenham College side, Joe Lister was selected in 1948 for the Rest against the Southern Schools at Lord's, where he scored 75 in eighty minutes. He made his first-class debut during his National Service with the RAF in May 1951, for the Combined Services against Glamorgan at Pontypridd. Lieutenant Lister was stumped by Haydn Davies off Norman Hever for 3 in the first innings and bowled by Hever for 8 in the second, his only appearance of the season. After demobilisation he joined Yorkshire and appeared for their Minor Counties side in 1953, scoring 385 runs at an average of 64.16, with a best of 103 at Nantwich against Cheshire. In 1954 he made his County Championship debut at Bristol, but left Yorkshire during the season to take up the post as assistant secretary to Major Bryan Bayley at New Road. Lister made his Worcestershire debut against Cambridge University that summer, finding himself in the unusual situation of playing for two counties in the same season, echoing what Major Jewell had done in 1919.

At New Road in 1955 he opened with 'Laddie' Outschoorn against Kent and was bowled by a slow full-toss delivered by Colin Page when he was just one run short of his century. In the next home match, this time at Chester Road, Kidderminster, his opening partner was Don Kenyon and they shared a partnership of 100. The season ended with Lister scoring 567 runs at an average of 23.62, his best season in first-class cricket. When he became joint secretary in 1956, a position he shared with Peter Richardson, he made only four more Championship appearances. He became secretary in 1958 when Richardson turned professional with Kent and when the Second XI Championship began in 1959 he captained the side in all their matches that season. In 172 Second XI matches between 1959 and 1971, he scored 2,852 runs, with a best of 143* at Northampton in 1962, the season he led Worcestershire to their first Second XI Championship title. All this time he carried on with his duties in the office, organised a Worcestershire tour of seven countries covering 34,000 miles in early 1965 and was an astute follower of matters of the equine industry.

When Jack Nash retired as secretary of Yorkshire in 1971, Lister was chosen as his replacement, a position he held until his death in 1991.

Gordon Lord

LHB & SLA, 1987-91

Born: Edgbaston, Birmingham, 25 April 1961

Batting career:

M	I	NO	Runs	Av	50
67	111	8	2898	28.13	16
12	*12*	*0*	*175*	*14.85*	*1*

100	Ct/St
4	16
-	*1*

Bowling career:

O	M	R	W	Av	5wI	10wM
2	0	24	0	-	-	-

Career best performances:

190 v. Hampshire, Worcester, *1990*

78 v. Northamptonshire, Worcester, 1990

Gordon Lord scored 823 runs and took 55 wickets for Warwick School in 1979, a performance which gained him selection for the England Young Cricketers' tour of the West Indies the following winter, where he played in the three 'Tests'. He had already appeared for Warwickshire in the Second XI Championship, having made his debut in 1977 when just sixteen years old. He made his first-class debut for Warwickshire at Trent Bridge in August 1983, scoring 61 in the first innings and 29 in the second. Lord scored his maiden century in a memorable match at Edgbaston in 1985, when Geoff Boycott hit his 100th hundred for Yorkshire and Dennis Amiss his 96th in first-class cricket. In a partnership of 206 for the second wicket with Alvin Kallicharran, Lord scored 199 off 252 balls, with 4 sixes and 29 fours, and was run out going for a second run that would have given him a double-century. He left Warwickshire to join Worcestershire at the end of the 1986 season, having made just 18 appearances there, and made his debut against Somerset in 1987 during Ian Botham's triumphant return to Taunton. Lord opened with Tim Curtis and scored 29 out of a 60 partnership before he was run out. Rain destroyed the match but not before Botham had scored 126 not out off 111 balls.

During Worcestershire's Championship-winning season of 1988, Lord opened the innings regularly and at Bristol, the last away game of the season, he scored 101, batting throughout the innings and being last out when he was David Graveney's fourteenth victim of the match. He finished the season with 862 runs at an average of 27.80, had a moderate season in 1989 but scored 1,003 runs in 1990, hitting three centuries. The best of these was at New Road against Hampshire, where he hit 190, sharing partnerships of 167 with Tim Curtis for the first wicket and 166 for the second with Graeme Hick. He struck 2 sixes and 29 fours during his five and a half hours innings, his second century in four days following his 101 against Lancashire at Kidderminster.

Lord made just four appearances in the Sunday League side, three of them in 1990 when he scored 78 at New Road against Northamptonshire. He shared an opening partnership of 116 with Curtis and hit 3 sixes, one each off Wayne Larkins, Nick Cook and Tony Penberthy. He left at the end of the 1991 season and is currently ECB coach education manager, based at Edgbaston.

Charles Lyttelton
RHB & RM, 1932-39

Born: London, 8 August 1909
Died: London, 20 March 1977

Batting career:

M	I	NO	Runs	Av	50
93	152	14	2708	19.62	12

100	Ct/St
1	47

Bowling career:

O	M	R	W	Av	5wl	10wM
329.3	41	1250	32	39.06	-	-

Career best performances:

162 v. Leicestershire, Loughborough, 1938
4-83 v. South Africans, Worcester, 1935

Charles Lyttelton was the last of the long line of this famous cricketing family to play first-class cricket. He followed his father, John (1924-25), and his uncle, Charles (1906-10), in the Worcestershire side for whom he made his debut against Gloucestershire at New Road in 1932, his only appearance that season. At Dudley in 1934, three Gloucestershire batsmen scored centuries in a total of 625 for 6 declared, with Charlie Barnet scoring 170, Charles Dacre 104 and Wally Hammond 265 not out (my father saw some of this Hammond innings and when I was born in the October of that year I was given the name Walter as one of my Christian names). Worcestershire began their second innings 299 runs behind and, despite a sixth wicket partnership between Dick Howorth and Lyttelton of 121, they lost by an innings and 34 runs with Tom Goddard taking 7 second innings wickets for 105.

The Worcestershire captain, Cyril Walters, was injured during the match with Essex at New Road in early June 1935 and appeared on just two more occasions that season, at the end of which he retired. Lyttelton took over the captaincy, a post he held until the beginning of

the Second World War. He was an enthusiastic and inspiring leader and was held in the greatest affection by those he led. At Loughborough in 1938 he scored a career-best score of 162, which helped Worcestershire to a first innings total of 501 for 9 declared. He hit 4 sixes and 15 fours and shared a partnership of 113 in forty minutes with Syd Buller, which is still the best for the Worcestershire eighth wicket against Leicestershire. Four wickets each by Roly Jenkins and Howorth left Worcestershire needing fifteen runs to win, which they managed with the loss of Charlie Bull's wicket.

Lyttelton did not return to first-class cricket after the war, by which time he had become the tenth Viscount Cobham on the death of his father in 1949. In 1954 he was elected president of the MCC and was its treasurer between 1963 and 1964, on his return from New Zealand where he had been Governor-General from 1957 until 1962. Whilst he held this post he played his last first-class match for his eleven against the touring MCC side at Auckland in February 1961, scoring 44 and 13.

He was elected president of Worcestershire at the 1977 AGM on 14 March but he died suddenly a week later. No one ever enjoyed his cricket more or took more trouble to see that others enjoyed theirs.

Glen McGrath
RHB & RF, 2000

Born: Dubbo, New South Wales, Australia, 9 February 1970

Batting career:

M	I	NO	Runs	Av	50
14	15	3	112	9.33	1
17	8	4	2	0.50	-

100	Ct/St
-	3
-	-

Bowling career:

O	M	R	W	Av	5wl	10wM
415.4	132	1057	80	13.21	6	3
134.4	34	311	34	9.14	-	-

Career best performances:

55 v. Nottinghamshire, Worcester, 2000
1* v. Gloucestershire, Worcester, 2000
8-41 v. Northamptonshire, Worcester, 2000
4-9 v. Yorkshire, Worcester, 2000

Glenn McGrath was the Worcestershire overseas replacement when Tom Moody returned to Australia at the end of the 1999 season. Much was expected of him and he never let anyone down, as was proved by his 80 first-class wickets at an average of 13.21, the most wickets by any bowler in 2000 – he was taking a wicket every 31.17 balls. He also performed heroics in the one-day competitions and his National League figures were truly incredible with 30 wickets at an average of 8.13. That average was the best ever in the competition, for any bowler with more than 15 wickets in the season, beating the 8.63 by Leicestershire's James Ormond in 1998, and the economy rate is more impressive. During the inaugural season of the Sunday League in 1969, batsmen were learning how to approach the forty-overs game and bowlers were generally on top. At the end of that first season Derek Shackleton had bowled 104 overs at 2.230 runs per over and last season McGrath bowled 112.4 overs at 2.165.

When McGrath arrived at New Road he came with three ten wickets in a match performances. By the end of the season had doubled this achievement ending with his best of 12-116 against Northamptonshire at New Road, having had career-best figures of 8 for 41 in their second innings; at Edgbaston, when he had Anuarag Singh caught by Staurt Lampitt, he completed 500 first-class wickets.

McGrath had a memorable day with the bat when he scored his maiden fifty, 55 at New Road, sharing a last wicket partnership of 103 with Kabir Ali. This was a Worcestershire record for that wicket against Nottinghamshire and only their third ever hundred partnership for the tenth wicket.

International call-up for the indoor tournament in Australia in August caused him to miss three Championship matches and two in the League, but the biggest disappointment of the season was the outcome of the NatWest Trophy when they had beaten Gloucestershire at New Road in the first round. In the first meeting he bowled ten overs for 23 runs and in the replay, which came about because of an administration error, he took 4 for 23 off his ten but Gloucestershire went through by five runs.

When McGrath returned home to a Test career of 288 wickets at an average of 22.42, he left village life in Worcestershire, with his English-born wife Jane. He had spent a most agreeable time in Martley, for whose village side he appeared against Worcestershire in a benefit match for Lampitt.

Sid Martin
RHB & RM, 1931-39

Born: Durban, South Africa, 11 January 1909
Died: South Africa, February 1988

Batting career:

M	I	NO	Runs	Av	50
236	405	26	9993	26.36	54

100	Ct/St
13	151

Bowling career:

O	M	R	W	Av	5wl	10wM
4973.2	1112	13358	459	29.10	18	5

Career best performances:

191* v. Northamptonshire, Worcester, 1935
8-24 v. Sussex, Worcester, 1939

Sid Martin made his Worcestershire debut against the 1931 touring New Zealanders having made his first-class debut for his native Natal in the 1925/26 season in South Africa. At the end of his first full season he was close to completing 1,000 runs, just 42 short; but during the following seven seasons he always reached this target and in 1937 and 1939 added over 100 wickets to those runs. He scored his maiden first-class century at Edgbaston in 1932, 116 in three hours with a five and 12 fours, and he appeared in all of the 29 matches. Martin showed remarkable fitness and form during his stay with Worcestershire, playing in every match in six of his eight full seasons, including an unbroken run between 1934 and 1937. Against Northamptonshire at Stourbridge in 1934 he shared the best of his partnerships with 'Doc' Gibbons, one of 279 for the third wicket, hitting 150 in four hours with 2 sixes and 15 fours, the partnership lasting 235 minutes. He seemed enjoy his battles with Northamptonshire more than any other county, scoring 849 runs at an average of 42.45, with another two centuries added to

this one at Stourbridge in 1934, including his career best in 1935. At New Road he came to the crease when the first wicket fell at 14 and remained until last man 'Peter' Jackson was bowled by 'Nobby' Clark. Martin scored 191 not out in four hours and forty minutes and added 79 in 35 minutes for the last wicket with Jackson.

During his last season with Worcestershire he achieved his best innings and match bowling performances. At New Road against Sussex he took 8 for 24, with 5 for 64 in the second innings. He helped Worcestershire to an innings win against Kent at Gillingham with match figures of 14 for 107 (6 for 23 and 8 for 84). In the next match he hit 102 not out in an unbroken fifth wicket partnership of 207 with Gibbons, which led to a six wickets win.

Martin played for Natal and Rhodesia after the war, finishing at the end of the 1949/50 season with a career aggregate of 11,511 runs and 532 wickets. His nephew, Hugh Tayfield, became a respected off-spinner for South Africa in 37 Test Matches. His son, Hugh, played for Transvaal and New South Wales, having spent 1965 and 1966 with Worcestershire Second XI, scoring 729 runs at an average of 17.35 and taking 49 wickets at an average of 20.65.

Tom Moody

RHB & RM, 1991-99

Born: Adelaide, Australia, 2 October 1965

Batting career:

M	I	NO	Runs	Av	50
120	197	19	8943	50.24	36
159	*155*	*19*	*6599*	*48.52*	*43*

100	Ct/St
22	141
15	*57*

Bowling career:

O	M	R	W	Av	5wI	10wM
1240.2	318	3919	118	33.21	5	1
676	*74*	*2533*	*102*	*24.83*	*-*	*-*

Career best performances:

212 v. Nottinghamshire, Worcester, 1996
180 v. Surrey, The Oval, 1994*
7-92 v. Gloucestershire, Worcester, 1996
4-24 v. Scotland, Worcester, 1998

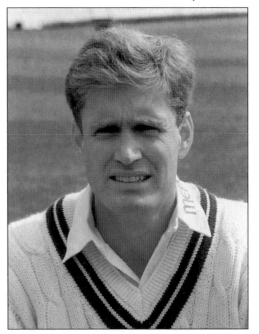

Tom Moody joined Worcestershire as their overseas player for 1991, following the English qualification of Graeme Hick and the fact that Warwickshire had made the decision to continue with Allan Donald. He made the most incredible debut for the county in a Sunday League game at New Road where he scored 160 from 111 balls against Kent, the highest innings in the competition for a first appearance for a county. In the next game he scored 128 not out in a ten wickets win at Bristol, followed by 50 against Lancashire and 100 at Northampton. At the end of the season he had hit 917 runs, a competition record. His form, not surprisingly, continued in first-class matches. His best season for Worcestershire was in 1991, when he scored 1,887 runs at an average of 62.90 and hit six centuries, including his career best.

At Ilford he shared an unbroken second wicket partnership of 264 with Tim Curtis, scoring 181 not out, hitting 6 sixes and 18 fours, but his highest partnership was with Graeme Hick at Southampton in the last match of the 1997 season. When Moody joined Hick the score was 100 for 2, and when he declared they had added 438, the highest partnership by a pair of Worcestershire batsman and a record for the third wicket in the County Championship. They were watched by Tom Graveney and Martin Horton, who held the previous Worcestershire third wicket record of 314 against Somerset in 1962.

When Worcestershire won the NatWest Trophy in 1994, Moody won man of the match awards in the semi-final and in the final. At The Oval in the semi-final he scored 180 off 160 deliveries, the highest innings against a first-class county in the history of the competition. When Surrey batted he took a catch on the boundary edge to stop Joey Benjamin hitting his third six off Stuart Lampitt in the last over of the match, giving his side a seven runs win with one ball remaining. In the final against Warwickshire he bowled 12 overs for 17 runs, and hit 88 not out in an unbroken match-winning partnership of 198 with Hick for the third wicket.

During his short Warwickshire career he hit a century off 36 balls in 26 minutes against Glamorgan at Swansea in 1990 and led Western Australia to two Sheffield Shield titles. He was a member of the Australian World Cup winning side in 1999, but eight Test appearances seems small reward for such a fine cricketer. Moody returns to New Road in 2001 to take over has head coach, after Bill Athey's departure at the end of the 2000 season.

Phil Neale
RHB & RM, 1975-92

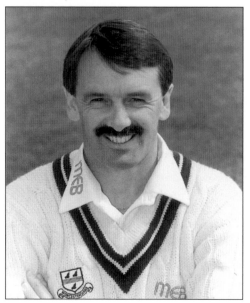

Born: Scunthorpe, Lincolnshire, 5 June 1954

Batting career:

M	I	NO	Runs	Av	50
353	569	91	17431	36.46	89
332	*300*	*63*	*7159*	*30.24*	*32*

100	Ct/St
28	132
2	*88*

Bowling career:

O	M	R	W	Av	5wl	10wM
78.4	5	369	2	184.50	-	-
8.2	*0*	*50*	*2*	*25.00*	*-*	*-*

Career best performances:

167 v. Sussex, Kidderminster, 1988

128 v. Lancashire, Old Trafford, 1980

1-15 v. Derbyshire, Worcester, 1976

2-46 v. Warwickshire, Worcester, 1976

Phil Neale made his first appearance for Worcestershire in a Second XI Championship match at Stourbridge in 1972 against Derbyshire. He had had trials with Nottinghamshire and Northamptonshire and had played Bradford League cricket with Pudsey St Lawrence when he was at Leeds University. He left university in 1975 with an honours degree in Russian and was offered a contract with Worcestershire and, at the same time, was signed by Graham Taylor for Lincoln City. He made his debut at Swindon in January 1975 when he replaced Dick Krzywicki during an FA Cup third round game and in June that same year he made his first-class debut at New Road against Oxford University. During that season he made his Sunday League debut at Old Trafford in a match that ended in a tie when he and his partner, Norman Gifford, scrambled a leg-bye off the last ball to level the scores. There was a happier return there in the Benson & Hedges Cup in 1980 when he hit 128, sharing a partnership of 191 with Glenn Turner, a Worcestershire record for the second wicket in that competition.

Success arrived quickly on the soccer field with 'The Imps', winning the Fourth Division with a record number of points and goals in 1975/76 and he eventually made 335 League

appearances, scoring 22 goals, being the last of the regular cricket/soccer full-time sportsmen. He was not quite the last first-class cricketer to play in the Football League, however; this honour goes to Tony Cottey, the Glamorgan and Sussex batsman, who came on as a substitute for Swansea City at Vetch Field against Bristol Rovers on 11 May 1985, seventeen days after Neale had made his last appearance against Doncaster Rovers at Sincil Bank. During this soccer career, in 1982, Neale came close to equalling the Chris Balderstone double of playing cricket and soccer on the same day when he played at Oxford for Worcestershire and was due to appear for Lincoln at Craven Cottage in the evening, but the soccer was postponed owing to the weather.

Neale scored his maiden century in 1976, 143 against the West Indian tourists in four hours and twenty minutes, sharing partnerships of 105 for the third wicket with Dipak Patel and 114 for the fourth with Basil D'Oliveira. This first full season ended with an aggregate of 949 runs, the first of the fourteen seasons in which he scored over 900 runs, seven of them over 1,000, with a best of 1,706 at an average of 47.38 in 1984.

Neale was appointed captain for the 1982 season, at the end of which Gifford, Ted Hemsley and Turner left, and the side slowly developed into one of considerable effectiveness

under the new leadership. In 1987 the Sunday League was won with a repeat performance and Worcestershire won the County Championship title in 1988 and retained it in 1989. After six defeats in Lord's one-day finals, success was finally achieved in the Benson & Hedges Cup when Neale took a catch to dismiss Paul Allott off Graham Dilley with Lancashire 65 runs short of their target.

The best of his 81 century partnerships was one of 231 for the second wicket with Glenn Turner at New Road against Yorkshire in 1981. Neale scored 102, his second successive century, but there are two other stands worth a mention. At New Road in 1990 he helped Richard Illingworth add 220, the best sixth wicket partnership for Worcestershire against Nottinghamshire, and at Derby in 1988 Neale and Steve Rhodes added 206, another Worcestershire sixth wicket record against Derbyshire.

In 1989 he was rewarded with a well earned benefit and at the end of it he was the first Worcestershire cricketer to exceed six figures with a cheque for £153,005. He had three more seasons with the county and when he left he had captained Worcestershire in 228 first-class matches, a figure only beaten by Don Kenyon with 257. Between 15 June 1985 and 25 April 1988 he was captain in 70 consecutive first-class matches. All of his cricket, except one match for England 'B' against the Pakistanis at Grace Road in 1982, was played for Worcestershire and it was a sad day when he eventually left the club. He joined Northamptonshire at the beginning of the 1993 season as director of cricket. The following winter he managed the England 'A' tour to South Africa and in 1994/95 took the 'A' side to India. When Bob Woolmer left to look after the South Africans, Neale was appointed coach at Edgbaston in March 1995, staying for five seasons with Warwickshire. Neale managed the England tour of South Africa in the 1999/2000 winter and was then appointed operations manager, with day-to-day responsibilities to the England team.

He still lives in Worcester with his wife, Christine, whom he married in 1976, and their children Kelly, aged twenty-one, and Craig, aged eighteen.

Phil Newport
RHB & RFM, 1982-99

Born: High Wycombe, Bucks, 11 October 1962

Batting career:

M	I	NO	Runs	Av	50
273	315	91	5450	24.33	21
263	*117*	*42*	*830*	*11.06*	*-*
100	**Ct/St**				
-	70				
-	*48*				

Bowling career:

O	M	R	W	Av	5wl	10wM
7214.3	1506	22177	825	26.88	34	3
1976	*166*	*7679*	*311*	*24.69*	*-*	*-*

Career best performances:

98 v. New Zealanders, Worcester, 1990

28* v. Yorkshire, Headingley, 1998

8-52 v. Middlesex, Lord's, 1988

5-22 v. Warwickshire, Edgbaston, 1987

Phil Newport played his first Second XI game for Worcestershire in 1981 after impressing with Minor Counties appearances with Buckinghamshire. He made his first-class debut at New Road against the Pakistani tourists the following season. Studying at Portsmouth Polytechnic took up most of the 1983 summer but he joined the staff full-time for the 1984 season and took the first of his five in an innings performances with 5 for 51 at New Road against Warwickshire. When Hampshire were the visitors to New Road in 1986 they found an in-form Newport difficult to handle, when he had figures of 5 for 52 in their first innings and a season's best score of 6 for 48 in the second. He finished the season with 85 wickets.

After spending the winter of 1987/88 in South Africa playing for Boland, where he took 23 wickets at an average of 19.47 and hit a career-best 86 against Transvaal 'B', Newport had his best season in 1988. He took 86 wickets at an average of 19.53, helping Worcestershire win the County Championship title. During that season Newport helped Graeme Hick add 205 at New Road against Yorkshire, the best ever seventh wicket partnership for Worcestershire, with Newport unbeaten on 77 when Hick was dismissed and Phil Neale declared. Against Middlesex in June 1988 he took a career best 8 for 52 at Lord's when rain caused two innings' forfeitures and Worcestershire helped themselves to a 209 runs victory. His performances in this season impressed the selectors and he was chosen for the one-off Test with Sri Lanka at Lord's, taking 3 for 77 and 4 for 87. Two more Test calls came his way, Australia at Headingley in 1989 and, called away from the 'A' tour of Sri Lanka and Pakistan, Australia at Perth in February 1991, where he hit a Test career best 40*.

Twice during the 1990 season Newport was to come close to a maiden century. His first effort was against the touring New Zealanders when he was out two runs short of his century, having batted for three hours and ten minutes, hitting 18 fours. In the next game Essex were the visitors to New Road and a ninth-wicket partnership of 120 with Graham Dilley saved an innings defeat, with Newport last out, caught and bowled by Derek Pringle for 96.

Newport was awarded a benefit in 1998, from which he received £82,066, and he had one more season in 1999, when he took 31 wickets at an average of 24.09. This brought his final aggregate from all first-class cricket to 880 wickets at an average of 26.97. At the beginning of the school year in 1999 he joined the teaching staff at Worcester Royal Grammar School.

Maurice Nichol

RHB & OB, 1928-34

Born: Hetton-le-hole, County Durham, 10 September 1904
Died: Chelmsford, Essex, 21 May 1934

Batting career:

M	I	NO	Runs	Av	50
135	233	16	7480	34.47	38

100	Ct/St
17	63

Bowling career:

O	M	R	W	Av	5wI	10wM
313.5	33	1281	21	61.00	-	-

Career best performances:

262* v. Hampshire, Bournemouth, 1930
2-6 v. Yorkshire, Worcester, 1933

Maurice Nichol became the first Worcestershire batsman to score a century on his first-class debut when he hit 104 against the West Indians in 1928, sharing a second-wicket partnership of 207 with 'Doc' Gibbons, who scored 200*. He was qualifying that season and that tourist match was his only appearance, but he made an immediate impact in 1929, scoring 1,442 runs in the Championship with centuries against Warwickshire, 132 at Dudley, and against Hampshire, 137 at Bournemouth. In the latter match he shared a third wicket partnership of 197 with Gibbons.

The following season Nichol showed his liking for this Dorset holiday resort when he returned to Dean Park and scored a career best 262 not out, having been dropped when 62. He hit 33 fours and shared partnerships of 130 for the fifth wicket with the Wolves full-back Vic Fox and one of 91 for the ninth wicket with wicketkeeper Bernard Quaife. The Bournemouth air suited Nichol again in 1933, when he scored his third century in four visits with 116, sharing a partnership of 256 with Cyril Walters, the best for Worcestershire's fourth wicket against Hampshire.

Nichol appeared for the Players against the Gentlemen at Lord's in 1931 and was selected as twelfth man for England at The Oval two weeks later against New Zealand, but that was all the representative cricket that came his way, even though he hit eight centuries and scored 2,154 runs in 1933. He finished off the season with that score of 116 against Hampshire, 165 not out against Glamorgan and 154 against Yorkshire in successive innings.

During the winter of 1931/32, Nichol spent several weeks in Sunderland Royal Infirmary, where he was seriously ill with pneumonia. This led to a loss of form and, by his standards, an unproductive season in 1932. He tired easily and failed to play a long innings of note. He was taken ill during his prolific 1933 season, unable to bat in the second innings at Leyton and missing the visit of Derbyshire in the next match. Even so it came as terrible shock when he was found dead in his hotel room on the Monday morning following the rest day in the match against Essex at Chelmsford in May 1934. He had played just five innings and scored 57 runs up to this fateful match at Chelmsford over the Whitsuntide weekend and on the Saturday had undergone a long and tiring day in the field, with Essex reaching 376 for 6 at the close.

Alan Ormrod
RHB & OB, 1962-83

Born: Ramsbottom, Lancashire, 22 December 1942					
Batting career:					
M	I	NO	Runs	Av	50
465	789	91	21753	31.16	105
268	*261*	*25*	*6119*	*25.92*	*33*
100	Ct/St				
31	384				
2	*71*				
Bowling career:					
O	M	R	W	Av	5wl	10wM
292	53	1064	25	42.56	1	-
25.3	*0*	*134*	*4*	*33.50*	*-*	*-*

Career best performances:

204* v. Kent, Dartford, 1973

124 v. Gloucestershire, Worcester, 1976*

5-27 v. Gloucestershire, Bristol, 1972

3-51 v. Hampshire, Worcester, 1972

Alan Ormrod was recommended to Worcestershire by their coach Charlie Hallows and he made his first appearance in the Second XI Championship at Newport against Glamorgan, at the age of sixteen, on the opening day of that competition in 1959. Two days after scoring 154 not out against Gloucestershire Seconds at New Road in July 1962, Ormrod made his first-class debut at Stourbridge against Lancashire, but he was bowled by Bob Barber before he had scored. During the two title-winning seasons of 1964 and 1965 Ormrod made 12 and 18 appearances respectively, but his maiden century eluded him until 1968 when, during his 230th first-class innings, he scored 123 at Portsmouth before he retired hurt, having hit 11 fours.

Ormrod completed the first of his twelve 1,000 runs in a season performances in 1966 and on the strength of this he was selected for an MCC under-25 team, captained by Mike Brearley, which went to Pakistan during the winter that followed. He hit one half-century, 61 not out at Peshawar against the Northern Zone, sharing an unbroken fifth-wicket partnership of 234 with Brearley, who hit a career best 312 not out.

When Ron Headley left New Road at the end of the 1974 County Championship winning

season, Ormrod was persuaded by Norman Gifford to open the innings with Glenn Turner and his career went up a gear. They shared 26 century opening stands together, three of which turned into doubles. At Northampton they added 213 in 1976, 254 at New Road against Surrey in 1978 and the best of the three, 291 in 1982 against Warwickshire. This last one, at New Road, is the third-best opening partnership ever for Worcestershire and their best against Warwickshire. It was the day of Turner's 100th hundred, scored before lunch on the first day by which time they had added 181 of their runs and the partnership was broken when Ormrod was dismissed for 79.

Ormrod carried his bat through an innings on four occasions, equalling the four of 'Dick' Pearson between 1912 and 1923. In 1975 he scored 66 out of 187 at Chelmsford, 36 out of 73 against Sussex at New Road in 1977, 126 in 1980 out of 219 at Bournemouth, having travelled from Cleethorpes the previous evening, and 63 out of 136 at Derby in 1983.

Ormrod left at the end of the 1983 season and played 27 matches for Lancashire in 1984 and 1985 and was cricket manager at Old Trafford between 1986 and 1991. He was head coach at Trent Bridge from 1994 until 1998 and is currently director of cricket for Hertfordshire.

'Laddie' Outschoorn
RHB & RM, 1946-59

Born: Colombo, Ceylon, 26 September 1918
Died: London, 9 January 1994

Batting career:

M	I	NO	Runs	Av	50
341	586	53	15257	28.62	79

100	Ct/St
25	276

Bowling career:

O	M	R	W	Av	5wl	10wM
628.2	147	1961	33	59.42	-	-

Career best performances:

215* v. Northamptonshire, Worcester, 1949
2-15 v. Lancashire, Blackpool, 1953

Outschoorn spent a very unpleasant three and a half years as a prisoner of war when, as a serving soldier with the British services in Singapore, he was captured by the Japanese. He suffered from harsh treatment, disease and never fully recovered from those hardships after his rehabilitation in Britain at the end of the war.

At New Road, playing against a Combined Services side that contained Don Kenyon, Michael Ainsworth and Reg Perks in 1946, Outschoorn was one of four players to make their first-class debut. He had spent this season with Kidderminster in the Birmingham League and joined the county staff in 1947, becoming a regular in the side until his retirement. On his return to Kidderminster in 1948 for the visit of Derbyshire he celebrated the award of his county cap with his maiden century, when he scored 100 not out in the Worcestershire second innings, having taken five catches in the Derbyshire first innings. By the last match of the season he had just reached his 1,000 runs and a visit to play Essex at Clacton was to bring down the curtain on 1948. In the first innings Outschoorn was dismissed one short of his century and in the second hit 110 not out, the nearest he came to two centuries in the same match.

Outschoorn scored the first of his two double-centuries in 1949 with 215* against Northamptonshire at New Road, hitting 2 sixes and 18 fours, sharing a third wicket partnership of 241 with Charlie Palmer. At the end of the season he had held 55 catches, a Worcestershire record until it was beaten by Dick Richardson with 65 in 1961

During the 1954 season Outschoorn began to open regularly with Kenyon and they gave Worcestershire some fine starts, especially with their 277 at Gravesend against Kent, still the best first wicket stand for the county against Kent. Outschoorn hit 1 six, 1 five and 13 fours in his 126, his best knock of the season. By the time that Outschoorn retired at the end of the 1959 season he had shared twenty century partnerships with Kenyon, eleven for the first wicket, seven for the second and one each for the third and fifth.

Outschoorn spent much of his time afterwards coaching in England, Sri Lanka and Holland. When the first old players' reunion at New Road was staged in August 1992, he was happy to be amongst old friends and colleagues again.

Charlie Palmer CBE
RHB & RM, 1938-49

Born: Old Hill, Staffordshire, 15 May 1919

Batting career:

M	I	NO	Runs	Av	50
66	114	7	3252	30.39	19

100	Ct/St
6	31

Bowling career:

O	M	R	W	Av	5wl	10wM
661.3	179	1844	49	37.63	-	-

Career best performances:

177 v. Nottinghamshire, Dudley, 1947

4-50 v. Yorkshire, Worcester, 1948

Charlie Palmer was first noticed when playing in the Birmingham League for Old Hill Second XI when just fourteen years old, and in 1938 he scored centuries in consecutive innings against Walsall and West Bromwich Dartmouth, adding 5 for 45 in the latter match. That same July he made his debut for Worcestershire at Bradford where, after his first innings of 10, rain washed out the second and third days' play, but by the end of the month he had recorded his first half-century with 56 against Leicestershire at Loughborough. At the time of his career at New Road, Palmer was a schoolmaster and consequently his appearances were mostly during the school holidays and he played just ten matches during that first season, scoring 205 runs at an average of 14.64. On his first appearance the following season he scored his maiden century at Dudley against Northamptonshire. During his innings of 132 he hit 19 fours and shared a fifth wicket partnership of 261 in two and a half hours with 'Doc' Gibbons, which is still Worcestershire's best for this wicket against Northamptonshire.

His next innings was at Cardiff and he scored his second consecutive century with 128 during a seventh wicket partnership of 101 with Hugo Yarnold. Sadly, when he was bowled by Bill Voce at New Road for nought, his last innings before the Second World War, he was seven runs short of his 1,000.

Palmer never reached that form again for Worcestershire after the war, although he did hit his best for them, again at Dudley, when he scored 177 against Nottinghamshire in 1947. He hit 21 fours and shared a second wicket partnership of 128 with Don Kenyon and a sixth wicket one of 135 with 'Roly' Jenkins. In 1948, when the Australians made their customary bow at New Road, Palmer impressed with 85 and 34 and although he made only seven more appearances and an unimpressive showing for the Gentlemen against the Players at Lord's, he was selected for the MCC tour of South Africa that winter. On this tour he scored 478 runs at an average of 34.14, with a best of 116 at Port Elizabeth against Eastern Province, but failed to gain Test selection.

At the end of the 1949 season Palmer became secretary at Grace Road and also captained Leicestershire until 1957. He was manager of the MCC party to the West Indies in the winter of 1953/54 and made his only Test appearance at Barbados, scoring 22 and 0. Palmer has been president of Leicestershire, president of the MCC in 1978/79, chairman of the Cricket Council and chairman of the TCCB. He is an active member of Worcestershire Old Players' Association of whom he was president between 1993 and 1995.

Nawab of Pataudi

RHB, 1932-38

Born: Pataudi, Punjab, India, 16 March 1910
Died: New Delhi, India, 5 January 1952

Batting career:

M	I	NO	Runs	Av	50
37	64	7	2860	50.17	11

100	Ct/St
8	20

Bowling career:

O	M	R	W	Av	5wl	10wM
54	2	239	2	119.5	-	-

Career best performances:

231* v. Essex, Worcester, 1933
1-19 v. Warwickshire, Kidderminster, 1934

The Nawab of Pataudi joined Worcestershire in the summer of 1932, having been at Oxford University since 1928, where he had gained blues in seasons 1929-31, and hit 238 not out at Lord's in 1931 in the match against Cambridge. His Worcestershire debut was against the Indian tourists in June and he scored 83 during a second wicket partnership of 126 with 'Doc' Gibbons, followed by two Championship matches at New Road and one at Stourbridge in August without much success. At the end of the season he was selected for the infamous 'Bodyline Tour' under Douglas Jardine and made 102 on his debut at Sydney and 15 and 5 in the second at Melbourne but was left out of the remaining Tests.

On his return from Australia, Pataudi was an immediate success in 1933 having his best season for Worcestershire with 1,582 runs at 51.03 including three double centuries, a Worcestershire record for one season, two of them in consecutive innings. The first of these three was at New Road against Kent, where he scored 224* and shared a partnership of 274, again with Gibbons, the best by Worcestershire against Kent for the second wicket. After failing in the first innings against Essex at New Road, Pataudi hit 231 not out and the stand with Cyril Walters of 182 for the second wicket saved the game, Worcestershire having been asked to

follow-on. On then to Weston-Super-Mare for his record third, where he scored 222 in a high-scoring drawn match sharing partnerships of 116 for the second wicket with Charles Fiddian-Green and one of 151 for the fourth with Charlie Bull.

At New Road in 1934 he scored 214 not out against Glamorgan, the first Worcestershire batsman to have four double-centuries to his name and the only one until he was joined by Don Kenyon in 1956. Pataudi did not appear for Worcestershire in 1935 and 1936, just twice in 1937 and three times in 1938, when he hit the last of his hundreds, 121 not out at New Road against Hampshire. He was not seen again at New Road until he led the 1946 Indians on the opening day of the tour on a very cold April day when he won the toss and asked Worcestershire to bat.

His son, Mansur Ali Khan, also captained India and had an English career with Oxford University and Sussex, overcoming a serious eye injury caused by a road accident. Pataudi died suddenly while playing polo, one of the many sports he enjoyed, having gained blues at billiards and hockey during his University days.

95

Dipak Patel
RHB & OB, 1976-86

Born: Nairobi, Kenya, 25 October 1958

Batting career:

M	I	NO	Runs	Av	50
236	364	31	9734	29.23	40
200	*183*	*17*	*3559*	*21.43*	*11*

100	Ct/St				
16	132				
1	*50*				

Bowling career:

O	M	R	W	Av	5wl	10wM
4647	1202	13089	357	36.66	12	-
963.3	*65*	*4162*	*134*	*31.05*	*-*	*-*

Career best performances:

197 v. Cambridge University, Worcester, 1984

125 v. Hampshire, Southampton, 1982

7-46 v. Lancashire, Worcester, 1982

5-27 v. Northamptonshire, Worcester, 1982

Dipak Patel made his Second XI debut for Worcestershire in 1975, aged 16 years and 195 days, having joined the club via West Bromwich Dartmouth, his family having arrived in West Bromwich from Kenya in 1967. In 1976 he made his first-class debut and in his second appearance he became the youngest Worcestershire batsman to score a century. He was 17 years and 215 days old when he scored 100* in the Parks against Oxford University, sharing a sixth wicket partnership of 227 with Ted Hemsley. This remained a Worcestershire record for that wicket until it was beaten by Graeme Hick and Steve Rhodes at Taunton in 1988. Later that year he scored the first of his thirteen Championship hundreds with 107 against Surrey at New Road and he finished the season with 648 runs at an average of 29.45 but his off-spin was hardly used, bowling just forty overs for his three wickets. In 1981 he completed 1,000 runs for the first time, as he did the following five seasons that he was with Worcestershire, with a best of 1,615 in 1983 at an average of 38.45.

At Southampton in 1982 Patel became the first to score a century and take four wickets in the Sunday League. He hit 125 in 107 minutes with 12 fours and a six, off Tim Tremlett, while adding 224 with Alan Ormrod for the first wicket, a record for the competition at the time. When Hampshire batted, Patel took the wickets of David Turner, Trevor Jesty, Mark Nicholas and Tremlett for 39 runs, completing a fine all-round performance in an eleven runs win, ending a run of six successive defeats.

During the winter of 1985/86 he played for Auckland and there started a change of direction for his whole life. Patel was often spoken of as an England cricketer but never got the call, except for two one-day appearances in 1977 for Young England against Young Australia at Arundel and Lord's. At the end of 1986 he had made the decision to emigrate to New Zealand, having married a New Zealander, and in February 1987 he made the first of his 37 Test Match appearances at Wellington against the West Indies. He was a member of their sides in the World Cup for 1987/88, 1991/92 and 1995/96.

In 1991, playing against the Northern Districts, Patel scored a career best 204 off 155 balls, sharing an Auckland record fourth wicket partnership of 280 with Jeff Crowe and also had figures of 6 for 117 and 4 for 116 in the same match. When he finally called it a day at the end of the 1996/97 season he had scored 15,188 runs at an average of 29.95, with 26 centuries, and had taken 654 wickets at an average of 33.23.

Dick Pearson
RHB & OB, 1900-26

Born: Brixton, Surrey, 23 September 1880
Died: Droitwich, Worcestershire, 10 November 1963

Batting career:

M	I	NO	Runs	Av	50
445	794	37	18496	24.43	82

100	Ct/St
22	161

Bowling career:

O	M	R	W	Av	5wI	10wM
8285.3	1761	24191	815	29.68	35	3

Career best performances:

167 v. Glamorgan, Swansea, 1921
8-42 v. Surrey, The Oval, 1907

Dick Pearson was christened Frederick Albert but was always known as Dick as far back as his early days on the Surrey ground staff, well before he arrived at New Road in 1900 to make his first-class debut. London County were the visitors, led by W.G. Grace, who was making his only first-class appearance at New Road, and in the second innings Pearson was one of his nine victims in the match. Pearson was qualifying this season and played in four non-Championship matches, but was a regular the following season, scoring 945 runs with a maiden century, 108 against Leicestershire, at New Road. It was 1909 before he reached his first 1,000 runs in a season, but his most memorable season, 1923, was when, at the age of forty-three, he completed his first double. He completed his 1,000 runs during his 103 not out against Sussex and went in to the next match with 99 wickets. Glamorgan were the visitors for the last Championship match of the season and Tom Morgan was the first of a 6 for 42 performance that completed the double.

At New Road against Gloucestershire in 1913 he opened the innings as usual with Fred Bowley and they stayed together three and a quarter hours and added 306 runs, just three runs short of the Worcestershire first wicket record, with Pearson having hit 9 fours in his 106.

Pearson saved his best bowling performances for matches against Surrey when, in 1907, he took 8 for 42 at The Oval, Dick Burrows and a run out denying him all ten. In 1914 at New Road he performed the hat-trick. It was the only one of his career and he needed no help from the fielders as he had Andy Sandham leg-before and bowled Percy Fender and William Abel with successive balls.

When he retired at the end of the 1926 season he had enjoyed a career of 26 years and 110 days, the longest of any Worcestershire cricketer.

There could not be a better tribute by a fellow professional to any cricketer than the one given Pearson by Fred Root in his 1937 autobiography *A Cricket Pro's Lot* in which he writes 'But for Pearson there would have been no Worcestershire County Cricket Club now. Many of the present players owe their ability to his coaching and advice by precept and example. He played for Worcestershire with a fanaticism associated with the knights of the religious wars. Cricket was, in that sense, his religion, Worcestershire his God'.

Reg Perks
LHB & RFM, 1930-55

Born: Hereford, 4 October 1911						
Died: Worcester, 22 November 1977						

Batting career:

M	I	NO	Runs	Av	50	
561	841	142	8485	12.13	13	

100	Ct/St					
-	226					

Bowling career:

O	M	R	W	Av	5wl	10wM
18063.5	3914	50857	2143	23.73	140	24

Career best performances:

75 v. Nottinghamshire, Trent Bridge, 1938
9-40 v. Glamorgan, Stourbridge, 1939

Reg Perks was the son of a former assistant to Fred Hunt at New Road and groundsman at the racecourse at Hereford who played in a match for the MCC at Crystal Palace, alongside Sir Arthur Conan Doyle, against London County in 1902. Perks junior had to qualify for Worcestershire for two years and finally made his debut sharing the new ball with Fred Root against Surrey at The Oval in 1930, where he had the prize scalp of Jack Hobbs for his first wicket and finished the season with 59 wickets. The following season, 1931, he performed the first of his two hat-tricks when he dismissed Kent's Leslie Todd, Brian Valentine and Tom Pearce with successive deliveries at Stourbridge on 4 June in a match that had been transferred from New Road because of flooding! That season he was chosen for the first of his three appearances for the Players against the Gentlemen, this one at Lord's, and after taking 81 wickets he was awarded his county cap.

Perks recorded his second hat-trick in 1933 at Edgbaston, where he bowled Reg Santall, Jack Smart and Harold Jarrett with successive balls but in his next over George Paine struck him for 22 runs (4.4.4.2.4.4) to win the match for Warwickshire by four wickets with four minutes left.

On the last day of the 1934 season at the United Services Ground at Portsmouth, Perks had Sam Pothecary caught behind for his 100th wicket, his first time for Worcestershire. He went on to this bowler's landmark for the next fifteen seasons, although in 1946 only 81 of them were for Worcestershire as he was still in the Army playing some matches for the Combined Services.

Continued good form in the late 1930s was noted by the selectors and Perks was chosen for the tour of South Africa in the winter of 1938/39 under Wally Hammond, making his Test debut in the Fifth Test at Durban. This is the most famous Timeless Test in the history of cricket, the longest first-class match ever played, ten days between 3 and 14 of March, and was left undecided when the tourists had to begin their two-day rail journey back to their ship at Cape Town. Perks took 5 for 100 in the South Africans first innings and 1 for 99 in the second.

Although Perks had had his best season for Worcestershire with the ball in 1939, taking 154 wickets at an average of 18.83, he was left out of the England side for the first two Tests against the West Indies, but was brought back for the third at The Oval, where he took 5 for 156 in their only innings in a high scoring, drawn match.

The Second World War took six seasons from his career and when it was all over he was thirty-four and Alec Bedser was on the scene. Perks consequently finished with just two Test appearances, but he continued taking wickets and was still bowling quite quickly. Towards the end of the 1946 season he took 5-54 at Cheltenham in the Gloucestershire first innings and in the second he had taken the first nine when 'Sandy' Singleton, the Worcestershire captain that season, dropped Colin Scott at slip off Perks to deny him all ten, only for Peter Jackson to then take the last wicket.

Perks was a typical tail-ender of the time who liked to hit the ball a long way in a short time, expressed clearly when he went in to bat against the 1949 New Zealanders at New Road. He hit 3 sixes and 5 fours in a quick fire 47 not out with one of the sixes, hit off leg-spinner Cecil Burke, carrying over the two rows of trees in New Road and thirty yards into Cripplegate Park, a hit of some 150 yards. By the time he retired he had scored more runs than any other Worcestershire batsman without ever recording a century, having a career best of 75 in 1938. At Trent Bridge he hit 4 sixes and 8 fours in thirty minutes, adding 84 for the last wicket with 'Roly' Jenkins, the best for this wicket for Worcestershire against Nottinghamshire until it was beaten by Kabir Ali and Glen McGrath in 2000.

By a strange coincidence, the United Services ground, scene of his 100th wicket in 1934, was an important venue for Perks once again. When he had Neville Rogers caught by Bob Broadbent in the Hampshire second innings he became the first, and only, Worcestershire bowler to take 2,000 wickets.

When Ronnie Bird retired at the end of the 1954 season, Perks was appointed captain, being the first professional to hold this position for Worcestershire. They struggled, finishing above only Glamorgan and Somerset and so an illustrious career came to an end with 2,233 wickets at an average of 24.07 in all first-class cricket. He became a car salesman and joined the committee in 1953, continuing until shortly before his death in 1977.

Cecil Ponsonby
RHB & WK, 1911-28

Born: Gravesend, Kent, 26 December 1889
Died: St John's Wood, London, 11 May 1945

Batting career:

M	I	NO	Runs	Av	50
74	127	26	784	7.76	1

100	Ct/St
-	73/11

Career best performances:
50 v. Surrey, The Oval, 1912

Cecil Ponsonby was educated at Eton but failed to make their eleven. Going up to Oxford he opened the batting in the Freshman's match but did not impress enough to play first-class cricket for the University. By then he had already made his debut for Worcestershire in 1911 at New Road against Leicestershire. He was deputising for the regular wicketkeeper Ernest Bale and took two catches in each innings and scored 31 not out in his only innings. This innings is still in the Worcestershire record books because he shared a partnership of 61 with Edward Righton, which remains their best for the last wicket against Leicestershire.

During the university holidays of 1912 Ponsonby made six Championship appearances. In the one at The Oval he scored his one and only half-century where he made 50*, but fine bowling by Ernie Hayes, who had match figures of 11 for 132, helped Surrey to a ten wickets win.

When Worcestershire returned to the County Championship in 1920, after a season of friendlies in 1919, Ponsonby played in three successive matches at Hove, Tonbridge and Taunton, with little success, once reaching double figures with 11 against Somerset. That

was the last seen of him that season but in 1921 he was around more than he had been before and kept wicket for the first time since his debut making 16 appearances, scoring 203 runs, and taking 16 catches and 3 stumpings. At Swansea he had his season's best score of 35, sharing a partnership of 105 with 'Dick' Pearson which was Worcestershire's best for the ninth wicket against Glamorgan until beaten by Steve Rhodes and Phil Newport in 1998. Ponsonby was appointed captain for the 1927 season in difficult times: Pearson had retired, Maurice Jewell made only intermittent appearances and Maurice Foster was available for only three matches. Thirty-three players were used in the Championship, twenty-two of them amateurs. One match was won, against Middlesex at New Road, seventeen lost and eleven drawn, with the match at New Road against Hampshire abandoned without a ball being bowled, and Worcestershire were left at the bottom of the table. Ponsonby scored 208 runs in 26 matches but the following season he handed over the captaincy to Jewell and made only one appearance, bagging a pair at Dudley against Nottinghamshire, and retired.

Of the 74 matches that he played for Worcestershire, he was on the winning side just seven times.

Charles Preece
RHB & RFM, 1920-29

Born: Broadheath, Worcestershire, 15 December 1887
Died: Oldbury, West Midlands, 5 February 1976

Batting career:

M	I	NO	Runs	Av	50
88	160	23	1575	11.49	2

100	Ct/St
-	53

Bowling career:

O	M	R	W	Av	5wI	10wM
1289.4	292	4037	135	29.90	5	-

Career best performances:

69 v. Sussex, Worcester, 1922
7-35 v. Essex, Leyton, 1921

Charles Preece made his debut for Worcestershire in 1920 against Hampshire at New Road, taking 4 for 38, bowling George Brown for his first wicket. He had made his first-class debut the season before, when he appeared for H.K. Foster's XI at New Road against Worcestershire. Worcestershire did not entered the County Championship this first season after the First World War and played nine, two-day, first-class matches; this was one of them and Preece had 2 for 75 and 3 for 62 in the match. At the end of his first season in the Championship he finished with 42 wickets at 30.11, with a best of 6 for 109 at Taunton.

On the opening day of the 1921 season at Leyton, Essex were bowled out for 90 in 90 minutes, with Preece claiming a career best 7 for 35, bowling unchanged throughout the innings. Things were a little different in their second innings when Essex scored 560 for 5 declared, Preece 0 for 113, with Worcestershire eventually losing by 132 runs.

In the drawn match with Sussex at New Road in 1922 Preece hit a career best of 69, sharing partnerships of 59 with John Coventry for the sixth wicket and 58 with 'Percy' Tarbox for the seventh. His previous best with the bat was 61 at Chesterfield in 1921, his only other venture into the fifties.

At Edgbaston in 1924 in the Warwickshire second innings he bowled Jack Parsons, then had William Quaife and Len Bates leg-before in successive balls to complete the hat-trick, the first by a Worcestershire bowler against their neighbours Warwickshire. He finished that season with 32 wickets at an average of 19.46, second to Fred Root in the Worcestershire bowling averages.

Preece virtually ended his first-class career at the end of the 1924 season except for a return to play one match at Trent Bridge in 1929 where he bowled three wicket-less overs for twenty-four runs.

After leaving he became groundsman for Chance Brothers, the glass manufacturers in Smethwick, Staffordshire and the details of his death were for some time confusing. He somehow got mixed up with a Ledbury-born Preece, Cecil Arthur, who died in 1966, whose obituary in the 1967 edition of *Wisden* stated that he was the Worcestershire bowler. Sometime later his son came forward in possession of the ball with which Preece had performed the hat-trick at Edgbaston and the correct obituary appeared in the 1977 *Wisden*.

Paul Pridgeon
RHB & RMF, 1972-89

Born: Wall Heath, Staffordshire, 22 February 1954

Batting career:

M	I	NO	Runs	Av	50
240	221	84	1188	8.67	1
226	*81*	*47*	*267*	*7.85*	*-*

100	Ct/St
-	82
-	*39*

Bowling career:

O	M	R	W	Av	5wl	10wM
6017.3	1256	17367	530	32.76	10	1
1702.3	*135*	*7060*	*218*	*32.38*	*-*	*-*

Career best performances:

67 v. Warwickshire, Worcester, 1984

17 v. Kent, worcester, 1972

7-35 v. Oxford University, The Parks, 1976

6-26 v. Surrey, Worcester, 1978

Paul Pridgeon played his early cricket for Himley before moving to Stourbridge in the Birmingham League and had trials with Worcestershire in 1971, joining the staff in 1972 when he made his first-class debut at Fenner's. He took his first wickets in the second innings of his Championship debut at New Road against Leicestershire, having figures of 3 for 50, bowling Barry Dudleston for the first of them. Brian Brain and Keith Wilkinson were released at the end of the 1975 season and Jim Cumbes had a summer playing soccer in the United States, so Pridgeon had more opportunities in 1976 and achieved his career best in The Parks against Oxford University with 7 for 35 and match figures of 10 for 94. That same season at Edgbaston he took a stunning caught and bowled to dismiss Rohan Kanhai in the Benson & Hedges semi-final, but for the fourth time Worcestershire fell at the final hurdle at Lord's.

In the Sunday League at New Road in 1978 against Surrey he had figures of 6 for 26 when the visitors were bowled out for 64 in twelve overs. These are still the best figures for Worcestershire in the league and in that competition Pridgeon took 167 wickets in 161 matches.

Pridgeon took 485 wickets in the Championship, with five-wickets-in-an-innings performances and a career best of 7 for 44 at Grace Road in 1987. During his best season, 1983, he took 72 wickets at an average of 27.47. In 1986 he took 66 wickets but after the arrival of Neal Radford and an improved Phil Newport, Pridgeon made only one first-class appearance in 1985, the farcical one at Fenner's when Worcestershire gave seven cricketers their first-class debut, three of them never appearing at that level again. He got back into the side in 1986, taking 59 wickets and helping Worcestershire to an innings victory over Middlesex at New Road with 6 for 52 in their second innings.

Pridgeon's popularity at New Road was proved when he received a cheque for £154,720 at the end of his 1989 benefit season and was a proud member of the County Championship-winning side that same season.

During the winters for many seasons Pridgeon was at the heart of the Stourbridge Football Club, as a fine centre-half and a possessor of a useful long throw. He also had a great love of National Hunt racing and was a member of a keen threesome with Norman Gifford and Ted Hemsley. When he left at the end of the 1989 season he joined the staff of Shrewsbury School coaching soccer and cricket.

Bernard Quaife
RHB & WK, 1928-37

Born: Olton, Solihull, Warwickshire,
24 November 1899
Died: Bridport, Dorset,27 November 1984

Batting career:

M	I	NO	Runs	Av	50
271	447	42	8498	20.98	31

100	Ct/St
3	175/54

Bowling career:

O	M	R	W	Av	5wl	10wM
36	0	231	5	46.20	-	-

Career best performances:
136* v. Glamorgan, Worcester, 1928
2-5 v. Leicestershire, Leicester, 1934

Bernard Quaife joined Worcestershire in 1928 after seven seasons with Warwickshire, scoring 1,096 runs, having played in the same Championship side as his father, William, on many occasions. On one occasion in 1922, the Derbyshire Bestwicks, father and son, bowled to the Quaifes at Derby. Quaife made his Worcestershire debut against Sussex at New Road and impressed with 77 not out, but the visitors won easily by 243 runs. He played in all the following matches, finishing with 903 runs at an average of 25.80 and scoring his maiden century. Glamorgan were the visitors to New Road when Quaife hit 136 not out, his hundred taking nearly four hours, but rain caused the loss of a day's play and the match was drawn.

At the end of the 1928 season wicketkeeper Francis Summers left Worcestershire; when the 1929 season opened Quaife took over the gloves for the first part of the season until Syd Styler made his debut in July. Throughout the rest of his career Quaife kept wicket in most of the games, taking 17 stumpings in 1935 and 14 in 1936. In the match at Portsmouth in 1936 he took two stumpings in the Hampshire first innings and three in the second, but towards the end of the season Syd Buller was qualified and Quaife was no longer required behind the stumps.

A match-saving partnership when Worcestershire were following-on against Middlesex at New Road in 1931 saw Quaife and 'Doc' Gibbons add 277 runs in 260 minutes, with Quaife scoring 107, his only century of the season. This is still a Worcestershire record for the fourth wicket against Middlesex.

Another partnership involving Quaife is still an inter-county record when he shared a stand of 211 with Syd Martin at The Oval in 1935, the best for the Worcestershire fourth wicket against Surrey. Worcestershire were in a follow-on situation again when Quaife joined Martin with the score at 74 for 3, still 202 runs short of making Surrey bat again. At the close of play on the second day they had added 144 runs and the partnership ended after two hours and fifty minutes with a lead of nine runs. The match wasn't saved this time and Surrey won by eight wickets.

Quaife reached 1,000 runs in a season twice, 1,021 in 1933 and 1,167 in 1935, scoring his third and last century in the latter season, 109 against Leicestershire. When Charles Lyttelton was absent through illness for a part of the 1937 season, Quaife led the side but he eventually retired at the end of that summer.

Neal Radford
RHB & RFM, 1985-95

Born: Luanshya, Northern Rhodesia (now Zambia), 7 June 1957					
Batting career:					
M	**I**	**NO**	**Runs**	**Av**	**50**
192	183	46	2126	15.51	6
218	*127*	*56*	*1502*	*21.15*	*2*
100	**Ct/St**				
-	79				
-	*61*				

Bowling career:						
O	**M**	**R**	**W**	**Av**	**5wI**	**10wM**
5537.3	1054	17749	653	27.18	33	5
1660.2	*155*	*6882*	*297*	*23.17*	*-*	*-*

Career best performances:

73* v. Nottinghamshire, Trent Bridge, 1992
70 v. Durham, Stockton-on-Tees, 1993
9-70 v. Somerset, Worcester, 1986
7-19 v. Bedfordshire, Bedford, 1991

Neal Radford appeared for Lancashire between 1980 and 1984 as an overseas player while playing in the Lancashire League, but arrived at New Road in 1985 English qualified. He played once for Lancashire against Worcestershire in a rain-affected match reduced to a one innings affair at New Road in 1981, where the home side won by seven wickets with Radford taking 0 for 27. However, in a Second XI match the following season he scored 108 not out at New Road and shared a unbroken fifth wicket partnership of 256 with Andy Kennedy, a record for that wicket against Worcestershire in the Second XI Championship.

Radford had an explosive debut season for Worcestershire, taking 101 wickets, his 100th in the second innings of the last match of the season against Northamptonshire, when he had Robert Bailey caught behind. He was the first Worcestershire bowler to take 100 wickets in a season since Norman Gifford in 1970 and he repeated this performance with 109 in 1987. When *Wisden* was published in the spring of 1986, Radford was named as one of their five Cricketers of the Year, a fitting reward for his 1985 season.

In between these two seasons, in 1986, he had career best figures of 9 for 70 at New Road against Somerset and the season's best in first-class cricket. At Edgbaston in July he was selected for England against India for the Third Test and took the wicket of Krishnam Srikkanth, followed in the same season by one Test against New Zealand at Lord's. The last of his three Tests was at Auckland against New Zealand in February 1988.

Radford usually wintered in South Africa, and he actually made his first-class debut there for Transvaal 'B' in 1978/79. He performed the hat-trick for Transvaal at Durban against Natal in the one-day Nissan Shield in November 1984, which was, at the time, only the second hat-trick in the fourteen seasons of the competition.

Radford was a formidable member of the Worcestershire one-day side, appearing in four Lord's finals and on the winning side in two of them. In the Benson & Hedges final of 1991, Radford struck 25 not out off Wasim Akram and Ian Austin during the last four overs of the Worcestershire innings and then took 3 for 48 off his nine overs.

When he ended his first-class career at the end of the 1995 season he was just six short of 1,000 first-class wickets. He was appointed director of cricket for Banbury and in 2000 led them to the Home Counties Premier League Championship title, taking 66 wickets.

Steve Rhodes

RHB & WK, 1985-present

Born: Bradford, Yorkshire, 17 June 1964

Batting career:

M	I	NO	Runs	Av	50
333	472	124	11480	32.98	58
356	*236*	*63*	*3132*	*18.10*	*3*

100	Ct/St
10	821/93
-	*400/95*

Bowling career:

O	M	R	W	Av	5wl	10wM
1	0	30	0	-	-	-

Career best performances:

122* v. Young Australia, Worcester, 1995
61 v. Derbyshire, Worcester, 1989

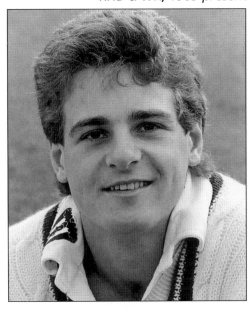

Steve Rhodes, one of Worcestershire's eleven Yorkshire-born wicketkeepers, made his debut for his adopted county at Lord's against Middlesex on the opening day of the 1985 season. Between 1981 and 1984 he had made three appearances for Yorkshire but, with David Bairstow their captain and regular wicketkeeper, the lack of opportunities forced Rhodes to move. He then played 97 consecutive games in the Championship, missing two in 1989 when he was selected for the England Texaco Trophy squad. By then he had been on the first of his five 'A' tours and scored his maiden century of 108 at Derby, where he shared a partnership of 206 with Phil Neale, a Worcestershire record for the sixth wicket against Derbyshire. Earlier that season he had shared another sixth wicket partnership – Worcestershire's best against Somerset – with Graeme Hick during his epic 405 not out, when they added 265 off 274 balls at Taunton, with Rhodes scoring 56.

Rhodes was an integral part of the Worcestershire side that won the County Championship in 1988 and 1989 and the Sunday League in 1987 and 1988. Indeed, he set an example behind the stumps that raised the standards of their fielding. In 1988 he took 70 catches and 8 stumpings, his season's best performance, with nine catches in the match against Sussex at Kidderminster, six of them in

the second innings. These nine dismissals equalled the Worcestershire record by Hugo Yarnold in 1949 against Hampshire and the six catches equalled similar performances by Rodney Cass (1973) and Gordon Wilcock (1974) – Rhodes has taken six catches in an innings twice since, in 1989 at Edgbaston and 2000 at Trent Bridge. Three years later, in 1991, Kidderminster was the venue where he shared the record Worcestershire eighth-wicket partnership against Derbyshire with Stuart Lampitt. When play began on the last day, Worcestershire were 110 for 4, still 44 runs behind, and with an early finish likely, spectators were charged a nominal 50p entrance fee. Lampitt joined Rhodes at 163 for 7, a lead of nine runs, and they added 184 and saved the game, with Rhodes scoring 90 and his partner 93.

New Zealand and South Africa were the tourists in 1994, the first time by the latter for twenty-nine years, and Rhodes impressed with a century at New Road against the New Zealanders early in the tour. Having been in Jack Russell's shadow for some time, he eventually replaced him, winning his first cap at Trent Bridge, scoring 49 and holding six catches in the match that England won by an innings. He kept his place for the other two matches

Steve Rhodes looks on as Warwickshire's Andy Moles is bowled at Edgbaston.

against New Zealand and was selected for the three against the South Africans, finishing with 222 runs at an average of 55.50 and taking 26 catches and 2 stumpings. This promising entry into Test cricket was rewarded with his selection for the winter tour of Australia. Here he played in all five Tests but without the same degree of success as in the summer and Alec Stewart replaced him behind the stumps when the West Indians toured in 1995.

Rhodes played in five Lord's finals, three Benson & Hedges Cup and two NatWest trophies, on the winning side in one of each. In the quarter-final against Northampton at New Road, on the way to the side's 1994 win over Warwickshire in the NatWest Trophy, Rhodes won his only man of the match award. He scored 24 not out, engineering a two wickets win in a low-scoring match, having taken four catches and a stumping in the Northamptonshire innings.

At the end of the Sunday League in 1988, the first four in the Sunday League entered a knock-out stage called the Refuge Cup. Worcestershire lost against Lancashire at Edgbaston in the first of these finals, but when the last one was played at Old Trafford in 1991, Rhodes opened the batting with Tim Curtis, replacing Tom Moody who had returned to Australia on international duty. Man of the match Rhodes scored 105, the only century made during the four year span of the competition, and Worcestershire beat Lancashire by seven runs.

Mention of the Sunday League, now the National League, conjures up a box full of wicketkeeping records by Rhodes. In 1986 he stumped four Warwickshire batsmen, three off Dipak Patel and one off Richard Illingworth, at Edgbaston, a record equalled in 1991 by Neil Burns for Somerset. He is the only wicketkeeper to complete stumpings against all other seventeen counties and the first and, as yet, the only one to complete 300 dismissals and take 50 stumpings. His aggregate of 336 dismissals is 79 more than the next on the list, David Bairstow, and his 72 stumpings leaves Bob Taylor's 49 well adrift.

One record in this competition that he does hold, however, is that he is the only batsman to aggregate 2,000 runs without having ever hit a fifty, his best being 48 not out on two occasions.

Rhodes completed his 1,000 dismissals in all first-class cricket during the 1999 season, but this is still 86 short of his 1,000 for Worcestershire, an aggregate reached only by Roy Booth, with 1,015.

Dick Richardson

LHB & LM, 1952-67

Born: Hereford, 3 November 1934

Batting career:

M	I	NO	Runs	Av	50
371	638	61	15843	27.45	87
11	*10*	*1*	*121*	*13.44*	*-*

100	Ct/St
16	415
-	*2*

Bowling career:

O	M	R	W	Av	5wI	10wM
90	10	322	8	40.25	-	-

Career best performances:

169 v. Derbyshire, Dudley, 1957
23 v. Essex, Worcester, 1966
23 v. Warwickshire, Lord's, 1966
2-11 v. Lancashire, Old Trafford, 1963

Dick Richardson made only four appearances in three seasons after his debut in The Parks against Oxford University in 1952. By 1955 he had become a regular in the side, scoring 848 runs and his maiden century against Gloucestershire at New Road in the last home match of the season, adding 116 for the fifth wicket with 'Laddie' Outschoorn. He was capped the following season and had the first of his eight 1,000 runs in a season performances, with 1,655 at an average of 30.81, and the value in his close-to-the-wicket fielding was also endorsed with 39 catches.

Richardson struck a rich seam of form early in 1957, scoring 101 not out at Bristol, 110 at Taunton, 115 against Essex at New Road and 169, a career best, against Derbyshire at Dudley. When the England side was selected for the Third Test against the West Indies at Trent Bridge, Richardson's name was there alongside Peter, his brother. Although he stayed seventy minutes and scored 33, this was his one and only appearance at Test level.

In 1961 Richardson held on to 65 catches, easily beating the previous Worcestershire best of 55 by Outschoorn in 1949. He also had another good season with the bat, scoring 1,774 runs with a match-winning innings of 165 not out against Surrey at New Road.

Worcestershire were chasing 373 runs to win when Norman Gifford joined Richardson with the score at 207 for 6. Two hours and twenty minutes later they had added 156 when Gifford was beaten by David Sydenham. Richardson soldiered on and, after four hours and fifty minutes and hitting 23 fours and 2 fives, Worcestershire won the game by three wickets with ten minutes to spare.

Richardson had his best season in 1962, scoring 1,825 runs at an average of 36.50 including three hundreds, and he held another 42 catches. The Championship-winning side was developing and he was an integral part of it, missing just two games during 1964 and one in 1965, when Worcestershire took the title in back-to-back seasons. He was awarded a benefit in 1967 and retired at the end of the season, having taken a Worcestershire record 415 catches. In the 1967 yearbook an appreciation of Richardson by the late John Arlott reads: 'If the cricketing quality of Dick Richardson had to be summed up in a single word, it would be "combative". He is one of those players of whom it is true to say that his figures do not reflect his worth'.

Peter Richardson

LHB, 1949-58

Born: Hereford, 4 July 1931

Batting career:

M	I	NO	Runs	Av	50
161	286	20	9118	34.27	51

100	Ct/St
15	82

Bowling career:

O	M	R	W	Av	5wl	10wM
46.3	9	178	1	178.00	-	-

Career best performances:

185 v. Somerset, Kidderminster, 1954

1-9 v. Northamptonshire, 1956

Peter Richardson made his debut for Worcestershire at New Road against Cambridge University in 1949, two weeks short of his eighteenth birthday, when he scored 39 and 35. He made his Championship debut that same season, but he really began to make his mark in 1952, recording two centuries. The first of these came in the Parks, where he scored 110 against Oxford University and the second, his first in the Championship, was 102 at New Road against Essex. Earlier that season, when Worcestershire met Essex at Romford, Richardson shared the first century partnership with Don Kenyon, 116 for the first wicket. They had 22 three-figure opening stands together, six of them in 1953, including 290 in just under five hours at Dudley against Gloucestershire. Richardson scored 148 and Kenyon 151 and when the latter was dismissed by Ken Graveney, they were just 19 runs short of the Worcestershire record partnership for the first wicket. By the end of the season Richardson had scored 2,029 runs, 2,295 at an average of 39.55 in all matches, his highest season's aggregate during his career.

The Army required the services of Richardson for his National Service in 1954 and 1955, but he was sometimes able to escape for an afternoon. On one of these occasions, at Kidderminster in 1954, he recorded a career best 185 against Somerset, hitting 19 fours and sharing another opening partnership with Kenyon, this one of 162

He made an explosive return to 'civvy street' cricket, with 130 not out at New Road when the Australians opened their 1956 tour. Worcestershire were following-on, 348 runs behind, and this five-hour innings saved the game with the score 231 for 9 at the close of play. Reg Perks retired at the end of the 1955 season and Richardson was appointed captain for 1956; he also shared the secretarial duties with Joe Lister. Richardson was selected for the First Test at Trent Bridge and had a remarkable debut. He scored 81 and 73, the first batsman to score a fifty in each innings of a first England v. Australia Test without reaching a hundred in either of them. Richardson played in 34 Tests, 19 of them during his Worcestershire career.

Joe Lister became secretary in 1958, Richardson being relieved of his joint role to allow him to concentrate on his responsibilities as captain, but at the end of the season Richardson asked for his release and he joined Kent as a professional, staying with them until 1965.

Born: Somercotes, Derby, 16 April 1890
Died: Wolverhampton, 20 January 1954

Batting career:

M	I	NO	Runs	Av	50
284	470	38	6772	15.67	22

100	Ct/St
1	189

Bowling career:

O	M	R	W	Av	5wI	10wM
12148.4	3718	28465	1387	20.52	121	33

Career best performances:

107 v. Kent, Worcester, 1928
9-23 v. Lancashire, Worcester, 1931

It seemed that Fred Root was destined to be a cricketer when his father moved from Derbyshire to become groundsman for Leicestershire at their headquarters, Ayelstone Road, in 1896. There he came under the influence of Tom Emmett, the Yorkshire and England all-rounder, who was the Leicestershire coach at the time and he joined their groundstaff on leaving Granby Road Board School. All-rounder Harry Whitehead was injured and just before the club and ground side left for a match in Derbyshire the Leicestershire secretary, Mr Rudd, announced that whoever scored the most runs in this match would replace Whitehead against Essex in the following Championship match. Root hit 79 out of a total of 130, but a young amateur was chosen instead and when the offer came to join Derbyshire, he accepted and joined them in 1910. He made his debut at The Oval, where he batted at number eleven, scored 6, and bowled two wicket-less overs for 12 runs. Before play began on the third day, however, the match was abandoned owing to the death of King Edward VII.

Root stayed with Derbyshire until the outbreak of the First World War, when he joined the Army and was posted to France. He was wounded in the winter of 1916 and at St Luke's Hospital, Bradford he received the grim news that he would not play cricket again.

He was invalided out of the army but proved the medical officer wrong, and played for Bowling Old Lane in the Bradford League until he returned to Derbyshire for a game against Lancashire at Chesterfield at the beginning of the 1920. By this time he had scored 927 runs and taken 63 wickets for Derbyshire, but he was then thirty years old and decided to qualify for Worcestershire. During this two year period he became the professional for Dudley in the Birmingham League and had a fine time. In 1920 he took 9 for 29 twice, against Mitchells and Butlers and Moseley, and against Stourbridge he scored 162 not out and took 6 for 70, taking over fifty wickets during the three seasons that he was at Tipton Road.

At the end of his first full season with Worcestershire, Root had taken 168 wickets at 20.25 with 16 five-wickets-in-an-innings performances and eight of ten in the match. Three of these ten wickets were taken in successive matches, the first at New Road, 10 for 204 against Northamptonshire, followed by 10 for 209 at Weston-Super-Mare and finishing off with 12 for 170 against Sussex at New Road. Despite these heroics Worcestershire finished two from the bottom of the Championship. In his book *A Cricket Pro's Lot*, a copy of which every modern day cricketer should keep in his 'coffin', Root states how much his skipper, Maurice Foster, encouraged him to experiment with his leg-theory, a method using seven leg-side fielders and bowling on a perfect length on the leg-stump.

Another good season in 1924 followed, with 152 wickets at an average of 16.01 and the first of his three nine-wickets-in-an-innings performances. At New Road against Essex he took 9 for 40 in their first innings with George Wilson, son of George (Worcestershire 1899-1906), taking the ninth wicket to fall. In 1930 he took 9 for 81 at Tunbridge Wells and at New Road in 1931 he took 9 for 23 against Lancashire, the best bowling figures for Worcestershire.

In 1925 he became the only Worcestershire bowler to take 200 wickets in a season when he had 207 at an average of 17.52, 196 of them in the Championship, taking five in an innings on 27 occasions and turning nine of them into ten in the match. Worcestershire, however, were only one place from the bottom of the table, Root having taken over half of their wickets, with Harry Rogers assisting him with 68. During the winter of 1925/26, Root toured the West Indies with the MCC party led by Frederick Calthorpe and he played in the three representative matches, the home side at that time having not yet attained Test Match status.

The Australians were the 1926 tourists and, on the strength of his 1925 form and his winter tour, Root gained selection for the First Test at Trent Bridge. His debut, however, was a miserable affair, with rain reducing play to just fifty minutes on the first day. England batted first, scoring 32 for 0, and Root never took part in the match. He was chosen for the Second Test at Lord's, missed the next but came back for the fourth at Old Trafford, taking 4 for 84 and that was the end of his Test career.

Root went in to bat at New Road against Hampshire for his last innings of the 1928 season needing 22 runs for his first 1,000 runs in a season aggregate, a target he reached quite comfortably, finally hitting 66. Having already taken more than 100 wickets that season, Root completed the only double of his career – although his batting was rather inconsistent. In

May, at New Road, he scored his one and only century, 107 against Kent, sharing a seventh wicket partnership of 107 with Vic Fox. Beginning with the visit of Derbyshire to Kidderminster in early August, he had a second innings nought, a 'pair' in the next match at Northampton and a nought and one followed at Cheltenham.

Root had a poor season in 1932, taking only 40 wickets at an expensive average of 30.75, and when he asked the committee for payment of his train fares from his home in Dudley to New Road and a winter payment of £164 it was decided that Root, at the age of forty-two, was no longer required. Following this decision not to retain him, Root wrote a letter to a national newspaper which caused something of a stir.

He went to Todmorden in the Lancashire League for a few seasons. Root joined the first-class umpires list in 1947, standing in the match between Northamptonshire and Warwickshire at Northampton for the first time, but after two seasons he joined his first county, Leicestershire, as their coach until 1950.

Root's autobiography A Cricket Pro's Lot was published in 1937 and following his time at Grace Road he became a respected journalist, working for the Sunday Pictorial. He lived in Dudley for the rest of his life and died at the age of sixty-three.

Born:	Stoneleigh, Warwickshire, 7 June 1875
Died:	Icomb, Gloucestershire, 2 October 1936

Batting career:

M	I	NO	Runs	Av	50
156	253	24	4335	18.93	17

100	Ct/St
3	92

Bowling career:

O	M	R	W	Av	5wI	10wM
2482.4	293	8099	362	22.37	24	1

Career best performances:

130 v. Oxford University, Oxford, 1911
7-54 v. Middlesex, Lord's, 1909
7-54 v. Lancashire, Worcester, 1910

George Simpson-Hayward made his first-class debut for Cambridge University in 1895 against the Gentlemen of England at Cambridge, his only appearance of the season. In three seasons at Cambridge he played on just three occasions, once in each season, and he failed to gain a blue. He was known then as George Simpson and added 'Hayward' in 1898. He made occasional appearances with Worcestershire's minor counties side prior to them joining the County Championship in 1899. His first appearance in the Championship was in the second game of that first season against Sussex at Hove and he played in another three matches with little success. During that season Worcestershire used five former Malvern schoolboys: three Foster brothers, William Lowe and Simpson-Hayward.

Simpson-Hayward missed the whole of the 1900 season but played more regularly in 1901 and 1902. During the latter season he took 5 for 11 with his under-arm lobs against Leicestershire at New Road, having taken 5 for 38 against Warwickshire there in the previous match. His 47 wickets at an average of 21.38 looked promising, but he was unable to play regularly until 1908, when he took 68 wickets and hit his maiden century. He was captaining the side at Oxford where he scored 105 and took 6 for 13 in the university's first innings and later that season

at Lord's he made the first of his two Gentlemen versus Players appearances.

Another good season followed in 1909, with 542 runs at an average of 21.68 and a career best of 7 for 54 at Lord's against Middlesex, and he was selected for the MCC party to South Africa for the winter of 1909/10. On his Test debut he took 6 for 43 at the Old Wanderers Ground, Johannesburg in the South African first innings, followed by 2 for 59 in the second. He took seven wickets in the Second Test and six in the Third, finishing the series with 23 wickets at an average of 18.26 – the matting wickets suiting his type of bowling – but that was the end of his Test career.

On his return he played eleven times in 1910 and repeated his career best 7-54 at New Road against Leicestershire, but 1911 saw him have his best season with the bat. He scored 795 runs at an average of 23.38, with a career best 130, made against Oxford University in two hours. At the Fox and Goose Ground, Coalville in 1913 he scored his only Championship century, 105 not out, against Leicestershire, an innings including 4 sixes and 12 fours, his last major performance for Worcestershire.

Doug Slade
RHB & SLA, 1958-71

Born: Feckenham, Worcestershire, 24 August 1940					
Batting career:					
M	**I**	**NO**	**Runs**	**Av**	**50**
266	376	98	5021	18.06	8
38	*31*	*6*	*268*	*10.72*	*-*
100	**Ct/St**				
1	178				
-	*8*				
Bowling career:					
O	**M**	**R**	**W**	**Av**	**5wl**	**10wM**
5294.4	2202	10761	469	22.94	12	1
96	*12*	*341*	*19*	*17.94*	*-*	*-*

Career best performances:

125 v. Leicestershire, Leicester, 1969

41* v. Hampshire, Dudley, 1969

7-47 v. Middlesex, Lord's, 1960

3-21 v. Glamorgan, Newport, 1964

Doug Slade made his debut for Worcestershire at Taunton in June 1958 at the age of 17 years and 301 days. It was an impressive start: his second ball in first-class cricket had the Australian all-rounder Colin McCool caught by Dick Richardson, finishing with 2 for 25 off 16 overs. At the end of this season he had taken 52 wickets at an average of 17.11, which puts him second in the Worcestershire bowling averages and twenty-second in the national averages. At New Road he bowled five Lancashire batsmen middle-stump to finish with 5 for 63. A quiet second season, which is often the way, was followed by his best when he took 97 wickets and scored 573 runs. He had his career best figures at Lord's when he took 7 Middlesex first innings wickets for 47, with another 4 in the second for a career best match analysis of 11 for 79 and a county cap to go with them.

During the winter he received an ankle injury playing soccer but played in the first two Championship matches before it was discovered that this injury was far worse than had been imagined and kept him out for the rest of the season.

He didn't get back into the 1962 side regularly until July and that month was unfortunate to be left on 99 not out at Gloucester, having shared a seventh wicket partnership of 101 with Roy Booth. At the end of the 1963 season he was chosen for a Commonwealth XI to tour Pakistan, playing in all three unofficial 'Tests'. In the first of these at Karachi he hit 74 not out and shared a stand of 161 for the eighth wicket with the West Indian quick bowler, Charlie Griffith; in the second at Lahore he took 6 for 126.

Slade was an important part of the Worcestershire attack that helped win the back-to-back County Championship titles of 1964 and 1965, taking 46 and 38 wickets respectively. His maiden century, however, wasn't scored until 1969 when, coming in as night-watchman, he hit 125 at Leicester, sharing a fourth-wicket partnership of 133 with Tom Graveney. Slade's batting was never really appreciated by Worcestershire, but when he left at the end of his 1971 benefit season he began breaking Birmingham League records with West Bromwich Dartmouth. In 1978 he hit a record 1,407 runs with seven centuries, the most ever recorded in the league, and he scored a record 972 runs in 1974 for Shropshire. Slade served on the Worcestershire committee between 1981 and 1992.

David Smith
LHB & RM, 1984-86

Born: Balham, London, 9 January 1956

Batting career:

M	I	NO	Runs	Av	50
56	87	13	3247	43.87	18
52	*52*	*10*	*1647*	*39.21*	*11*

100	Ct/St
8	32
2	*18*

Bowling career:

O	M	R	W	Av	5wI	10wM
17	3	57	3	19.00	-	-
2	*1*	*5*	*1*	*5.00*	-	-

Career best performances:

189* v. Kent, Worcester, 1984
126 v. Warwickshire, Worcester, 1985
2-35 v. Surrey, The Oval, 1986
1-0 v. Sussex, Worcester, 1986

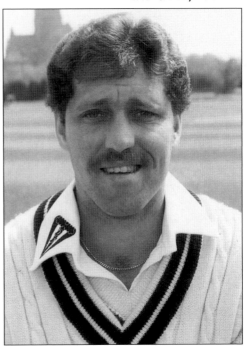

David Smith joined Worcestershire in 1984 after being asked to leave Surrey at the end of an eleven-year career at The Oval, where he was capped in 1980. Middlesex were interested in his services, but he was given a poor reference by Surrey and so the Middlesex's loss became Worcestershire's gain. Sussex were the visitors to New Road when he made his debut, scoring 23 and 53 not out, which helped Worcestershire to a six wickets win, their first ever Championship win in April. At the end of this first season he had scored 1,089 runs at an average of 42.03 and had a share of seven century partnerships. The best of his two centuries that season, 189 not out against Kent, remained his highest with Worcestershire and included 26 fours. The best of the partnerships was one of 153 for the fifth wicket with Kapil Dev against Hampshire. In 1985 he added another three centuries and scored 1,113 runs, the best of his three-season Worcestershire career.

During the winter of 1985/86, Smith was selected for the England party to tour the West Indies under David Gower. The tour began slowly for Smith, but he was chosen for the First Test at Sabina Park, Kingston, replacing Mike Gatting who had returned home with a broken nose. England were well

beaten by ten wickets and Smith made little impact with 0 and 1. He had a little more luck in the next match when he made his one-day debut at Port-of-Spain and was with Graham Gooch when England won by five wickets off the last ball. Gooch was unbeaten on 129 and Smith 10, and they had shared an unbroken stand of 47 runs. Smith was left out of the Third Test but returned for the Fourth Test, top scoring for England in both innings with 47 and 32, but a back injury while fielding kept him out of the last, ending his Test career.

Smith had another fine season for Worcestershire in 1986, but the sudden death of a business associate required him to spend more time in London and he moved back to Surrey. It was hardly a happy return and in 1989 he went to Sussex to finish out his career.

Motor racing was one of Smith's first loves and he bought himself a Mallock Clubman Sports and raced at Brands Hatch, Goodwood and Silverstone. In March 1995 he went one step further when he gained his pilot's licence.

Vikram Solanki

RHB & OB, 1995-present

Born: Udaipur, India, 1 April 1976

Batting career:

M	I	NO	Runs	Av	50
88	151	10	4988	35.27	27
109	*91*	*10*	*1740*	*21.48*	*7*
100	**Ct/St**				
8	100				
1	*31*				

Bowling career:

O	M	R	W	Av	5wl	10wM
717.2	144	2638	65	40.58	3	1
60.3	*0*	*321*	*7*	*45.85*	*-*	*-*

Career best performances:

171 v. Gloucestershirre, Cheltenham, 1999

120 v. Derbyshire, Derby, 1998*

5-69 v. Middlesex, Lord's, 1996

1-9 v. Sussex, Arundel, 1997

Vikram Solanki, raised in Goldthorn Park, Wolverhampton, was educated at Regis School, the same school attended by the Olympic gold medal-winning pentathlete, Denise Lewis. He first appeared for Worcestershire in the last Second XI Championship match of the 1991 season at Southampton, aged fifteen. When he made his debut in the First XI at New Road in the last Sunday League match of the 1993 season he was just 17 years and 171 days old, the youngest Worcestershire player to appear in that competition. In the winter of 1992/93 he went to South Africa with England under-18s and followed this with ten under-19 'Test' appearances with a best of score of 66 at Headingley against the South Africans in 1995.

Southampton was the scene for his first-class debut in 1995, where he scored a promising 30 and 31 and had Paul Terry for his first wicket. He appeared more regularly in 1996, ending the season with 828 runs at an average of 39.42. He had a career best bowling performance of 5 for 69 at Lord's but a more incredible match performance at Old Trafford. He took 5 for 116 and 5 for 140 against Lancashire and those 256 runs are the most conceded by a Worcestershire

bowler in a match.

In 1997, opening the batting against Oxford University in The Parks, he scored his maiden century, 128 not out. Even more progress was made in 1998 when he was unfortunate to end the season with 999 first-class runs, although he did score his first Championship hundred. It was rather overshadowed by Graeme Hick's 100th hundred; they shared a partnership of 243, the best for the second wicket for Worcestershire against Sussex and Solanki finished with 155, with 2 sixes and 24 fours, off 263 balls, their partnership lasting six minutes under four hours.

Solanki was selected for the 'A' tour of Zimbabwe and South Africa that winter and in the four matches that he appeared he scored 169 runs at an average of 33.80. The scene was now set for his best season when he topped 1,000 runs for the first time and went one better with his career best of 171 at Cheltenham, one of three Worcestershire century makers in a total of 591 for 7 declared. His 1,339 runs at an average of 40.57 was rewarded with another 'A' tour, this one to Bangladesh and New Zealand. On the first leg of the tour he hit a career best 185 at Chittagong against Bangladesh.

After another 1,138 runs at an average of 43.76, in 2000 he was invited to join England 'A' again for a season of Busta Cup matches in the West Indies.

Jim Standen
RHB & RM, 1959-70

Born: Edmonton, London, 30 May 1935

Batting career:

M	I	NO	Runs	Av	50
133	174	28	2092	14.32	2
25	*21*	*6*	*199*	*13.26*	*-*

100	Ct/St
-	83
-	*17*

Bowling career:

O	M	R	W	Av	5wI	10wM
3266.1	811	7934	313	25.34	12	-
176.1	*27*	*684*	*40*	*17.10*	*13*	*-*

Career best performances:

92* v. Oxford University, The Parks, 1970
31 v. Kent, Canterbury, 1970
7-30 v. Cambridge University, Halesowen, 1964
5-14 v. Surrey, Worcester, 1963

Jim Standen joined Worcestershire in 1959 after a season in goal for Arsenal and two seasons of Minor Counties cricket with Hertfordshire between 1956 and 1957. His appearances were limited until the 1961 season when he made 28 appearances, scoring 462 runs and taking 60 wickets with a best of 5 for 65 at Dudley against Hampshire. His soccer was at a lower profile, having left Arsenal, after 38 cup and League appearances, to join Luton Town. He was more successful with Worcestershire in 1962, having his season's best haul of 78 wickets, with the best of his three five wickets performances being 6 for 32 at Trent Bridge. West Ham United signed Standen in 1962 and when he took over from Lawrie Leslie at Hillsborough in December his soccer took a more prominent role and he played cricket less often.

In 1963 the Gillette Cup became a feature on the cricket scene. Worcestershire drew Surrey in the first round at New Road and won easily by 114 runs thanks to 5 for 14 and three brilliant catches, two off his own bowling, by Standen, a performance that won him the man of the match award. When Standen decided to sell his soccer memorabilia in 1994 at Christie's in Glasgow, this first Worcestershire Gillette medal was amongst the lots and went for £160, which

topped my postal bid by a tenner! Standen missed the final at Lord's, as on that same day he was busy picking the ball out of the net at Upton Park, where Sheffield United won 3-2. At the end of the 1963/64 he was at Wembley in the FA Cup-winning side against Preston North End in May.

After this memorable day Standen joined up with Worcestershire and completed a unique double by helping Worcestershire to the 1964 Championship title, taking 64 wickets at an average of 13.00, a tally that put him at the top of the national averages. Over the next three seasons he played little cricket and he kept a clean sheet at Wembley when West Ham beat TSV Munchen 2-0 in the European Cup Winners Cup in May 1965.

At the end of the 1970 season he called it a day, as he was now with Portsmouth by way of Millwall and owned two sports shops in Camberley. In October 1980 he moved to San Francisco where his wife, Elsie, became a highly-paid vice-president of an American bank – Standen had a personalised car number plate FACUP64.

Tom Straw

RHB & WK, 1899-1907

Born: Hucknall Torkard, Nottinghamshire, 1 September 1870
Died: Hucknall Torkard, Nottinghamshire, 5 September 1959

Batting career:

M	I	NO	Runs	Av	50
61	94	38	600	10.71	-

100	Ct/St
-	122/12

Career best performances:

32 v. Gloucestershire, Spa Ground, Gloucester, 1900

Tom Straw signed an agreement with Paul Foley, the Worcestershire secretary, as a professional cricketer at £3 per week for the 1894 season. Foley was instrumental in the establishment of the Minor Counties Championship in 1895 and Worcestershire were early front-runners, sharing the title with Durham and Norfolk that season and winning the competition in 1896, 1897 and 1898.

Straw was part of this success and when Worcestershire joined the County Championship in 1899 he was their first choice as wicketkeeper. He scored 130 runs at an average of 8.12, took 29 catches and completed one stumping. *Wisden* said of him 'Wherever he went Straw earned golden opinions by his smartness behind the stumps'. Straw was in the side for their first Championship match at New Road in May 1899 when Yorkshire were the visitors. He scored 9 in the first innings and 0 not out in the second, when Schofield Haigh bowled Bill Foster with Worcestershire twelve runs short of a famous victory.

However, his batting did sometimes cause problems. In the first innings of the match against Warwickshire at New Road, Straw hit the ball in the air and started to run. Alf Glover ran to catch the ball but Straw collided with him while trying to make his ground and he dropped the ball. Straw was given out for obstructing the field. In 1901, again against Warwickshire but this time at Edgbaston, he was given out again for obstructing the field, the only batsman to suffer this dismissal twice in first-class cricket and to this day no other Worcestershire batsman has ever been given out even once this way.

At the Spa Ground, Gloucester in July 1900, Straw hit a career best 32, adding 56 for the last wicket with Albert Bird and increasing Worcestershire's first innings lead to 74. Following this, George Wilson, with 7 for 76, gave Worcestershire the opportunity for a five wickets win in their first meeting with their neighbours Gloucestershire. Straw's only other innings of note was 28 at New Road against Warwickshire in 1901, when he helped Dick Burrows add 47 for the ninth wicket.

Straw twice took five catches in an innings, the first occasion being during the match of his first obstruction dismissal and the second in 1900 at New Road against Leicestershire. His best season behind the stumps was 1901, when he held 48 catches and took 8 stumpings. By this point, however, George Gaukrodger had arrived and Straw's appearances became less frequent until 1907, when he played his last game.

Percy Tarbox
RHB & RM, 1921-29

Born: Hemel Hempstead, Hertfordshire, 2 July 1891
Died: Peacehaven, Sussex, 16 June 1978

Batting career:

M	I	NO	Runs	Av	50
226	398	31	5824	15.86	19

100	Ct/St
2	122

Bowling career:

O	M	R	W	Av	5wI	10wM
4057.2	677	13256	375	35.34	11	1

Career best performances:

109 v. Nottinghamshire, Trent Bridge, 1927
7-55 v. Somerset, Worcester, 1921

Percy Tarbox is another of the Worcestershire cricketers who is better known by his nickname than his real one, Charles Victor. Almost thirty when he made his first-class debut for Worcestershire in 1921, his is another tale of a career that was delayed due to war. He joined the club at their lowest ebb and during his nine-season career, the highest that they finished in the Championship was fourteenth and they finished at the foot of the table on four occasions. During his first season he scored 629 runs, took 47 wickets and held 15 catches. In the memorable first first-class match at Chester Road, Kidderminster in 1921 he scored the first of his fifties, 62, sharing a sixth wicket partnership of 78 with his skipper, Maurice Jewell and having match figures of 5 for 38 which helped Worcestershire to a 38 runs win. In the side for that match was James Turner, the future father-in-law of the late Lord Runcie, the former Archbishop of Canterbury.

In June that season, at New Road against Somerset, he had his career best figures of 7 for 55. In the return match at Taunton he took 4 for 126 and 6 for 32, career best match figures of 10 for 158, which helped Worcestershire to one of their five wins of the season

Tarbox scored his only first-class century against Warwickshire in 1925, helping Worcestershire to their first win at Edgabston

for sixteen years. He came in first wicket down and was 103 not out in a total of 251, sharing useful partnerships of 76 for the fourth wicket with Maurice Foster and 51 for the fifth with Fred Root. By the end of the season he had scored 964 runs, his career best aggregate. Edgbaston was the scene for another of Tarbox's better batting performances. This was during 1929, his last season, when he helped former Wolves full-back Vic Fox add 141 for the ninth wicket in an hour and a half, the best for Worcestershire for this wicket against Warwickshire and their third best ever. Fox hit a career best 198 and Tarbox, the last of his half-centuries, 55.

Tarbox then had three seasons in the Minor Counties Championship for Hertfordshire, taking 11 wickets and scoring 328 runs and then spent six winters coaching in South Africa. He was on the first-class umpires list from 1937 until 1947 and renewed acquaintances with Worcestershire when he stood in a benefit match for 'Laddie' Outschoorn in 1959. His last job was cricket coach at the Royal Marines School in Bushey.

Glenn Turner
RHB & OB, 1967-82

Born: Dunedin, New Zealand, 26 May 1947					
Batting career:					
M	I	NO	Runs	Av	50
284	493	65	22298	52.09	93
247	*243*	*15*	*8471*	*37.15*	*52*
100	**Ct/St**				
72	241				
11	*95*				
Bowling career:					
O	M	R	W	Av	5wl	10wM
33	5	114	5	22.80	-	-
31.3	*3*	*148*	*7*	*21.14*	*-*	*-*

Career best performances:

311* v. Warwickshire, Worcester, 1982

147 v. Sussex, Horsham, 1980

3-18 v. Pakistan, Worcester, 1967

2-25 v. Yorkshire, Headingley, 1969

Glenn Turner was encouraged to come to England by 'Billy' Ibadualla, the Pakistani and Warwickshire all-rounder, who had arranged trials for him at Edgbaston. Shortly before leaving New Zealand he received a letter saying that they had no room for him as an overseas player, so he left and joined Worcestershire. He had already made his first-class debut for Otago in 1964 and he joined Worcestershire in 1967, played for Stourbridge in the Birmingham League, and made his debut at New Road against the Pakistanis. Don Kenyon was his first opening partner but they didn't spend much time together in this match, Turner scoring just 14 and 0. However, in the tourists' second innings he had his best Worcestershire bowling figures of 3 for 18.

Kenyon retired at the end of the 1967 season and Turner played a full season in 1968, scoring 1,182 runs, the first of his fourteen 1,000 runs in a season performances. He began batting at six but when he replaced Duncan Fearnley as Ron Headley's opening partner he became an immediate success. He had 59 and 71* against Leicestershire, followed shortly afterwards by his maiden century at New Road with 106*against Middlesex. The second half of the 1969 season was spent with the New Zealanders so he only made eleven Worcestershire appearances but returned for a record-breaking season in 1970. In 1933 Cyril Walters hit nine centuries but Turner went one better with ten, a record he held on his own until it was equalled by Graeme Hick in 1988, and he finished with 2,379 runs, his best season for Worcestershire.

The New Zealanders were back in England again in 1973 for the first part of a memorable summer for Turner. On 31 May he reached his 1,000 runs from 18 innings at an average of 78.30, only the second overseas batsman after Don Bradman to reach this target before the end of May. At New Road in April he scored 143 for the tourists against Worcestershire, which was to become a very important century later in his career. He rejoined Worcestershire at Cardiff in July and scored 109 not out in the second innings and finished with 1,036 runs and a season's grand total of 2,416 at an average of 67.11, top of the national averages. The following season, 1974, he scored the first of his six Worcestershire double-centuries with 202 not out against Cambridge University at Fenner's. On tour with New Zealand in West Indies in the winter of 1971/72, he scored four double-centuries, including his best in Tests with 259 at Georgetown.

When he went to Southport with Worcestershire in 1979 he had scored a century against every county except Lancashire,

including the one in 1973 against Worcestershire. At lunch he was 99 not out, having blocked the last four balls, but he took no chances this time, with his mind on the time that he was run out by Clive Lloyd in 1970 for 99. He went on to 109 and this century completed the first ever full-house against all counties, a feat equalled by Viv Richards in 1981 when he scored 128 at Taunton against Essex, having already reached three figures against Somerset for the West Indies in 1980. Both Turner and Richards scored two against every county except Worcestershire and Somerset respectively, but before the arrival of Durham in the County Championship.

On 29 May 1982 he became the nineteenth batsman to reach 100 hundreds and, at the time, only the second overseas player after Don Bradman. His 311 not out at New Road against Warwickshire was the first 300 runs scored in a day since Jack Robertson scored 331 at the same venue against Worcestershire in 1949. He had reached this milestone before lunch off 123 balls

in 114 minutes, with 2 sixes, one off a Gladstone Small bouncer and one off Jim Cumbes, and 13 fours. Ibadulla had time off from his umpiring duties and was at New Road to witness this innings. In *A Century of Centuries*, published in 1983, Turner said 'I was in the nineties for five overs but it did give Billy Ibadulla time to find the appropriate white waiter's coat to put on, and to make his appearances at the wicket with two double gin and tonics more authentic. They were large ones, without lemon of course, and my only concern, I suppose, was that the ice had melted'. When Worcestershire declared, he had beaten the county's previous best by Fred Bowley and batted for 342 minutes, facing 333 balls and hitting those 2 sixes and 39 fours. At the end of this season he left Worcestershire to return home with his wife, Sukhinder. They were married in June 1973, in between the end of the New Zealand tour and him rejoining Worcestershire. They had a Sikh ceremony in a temple in Southall, followed by a registry office ceremony in Brentford later.

Cyril Walters

RHB, 1928-35

Born: Bedlinog, Glamorgan, 28 August 1905					
Died: Neath, Glamorgan, 23 December 1992					

Batting career:

M	I	NO	Runs	Av	50
137	237	20	8193	37.75	34

100	Ct/St
18	62

Bowling career:

O	M	R	W	Av	5wI	10wM
63.3	5	335	5	67.00	-	-

Career best performances:

226 v. Kent, Gravesend, 1933
2-22 v. Northamptonshire, Worcester, 1933

Cyril Walters made his Glamorgan debut in 1923 and left to join Worcestershire as their secretary in 1928. He had to qualify for two years before he could play in the Championship, but he made his debut against the West Indies on their first visit to New Road, having already played in the Championship for Glamorgan that season. Hundreds by 'Doc' Gibbons, Maurice Nichol and Vic Fox saw that Walters didn't get to the crease and he had to wait until the visit of the 1930 Australians before his first knock. He was stumped off Clarrie Grimmett for 21 and then had to watch Don Bradman score the first of his three double-centuries at New Road. However, in July Walters scored his first Worcestershire century, 157 not out at Northampton.

Walters was appointed captain in 1931, having led the side in all but 10 of their 29 matches in 1930, but by far his best seasons were 1933 and 1934. He finished 1933 with 2,292 runs at an average of 53.30 including, at the time, a record nine centuries with a career best 226 at Gravesend, sharing a partnership of 260 with Charlie Bull, Worcestershire's best for the fourth wicket against Kent. Other partnerships that season that are still Worcestershire records

are the 256 with Maurice Nichol for the fourth wicket against Hampshire, 225 for the first wicket with Gibbons against Lancashire, equalled by Tim Curtis and Paul Bent in 1991, and 181 for the first wicket with Gibbons against Sussex. This form won him selection for his Test debut at Lord's against the West Indies in 1933, where he scored 51 in an innings win for England, and a trip to India with the MCC party under Douglas Jardine.

When the Australians opened their Ashes series at Trent Bridge in 1934, Walters captained England in the absence of Bob Wyatt. He appeared in all five Tests and ended his eleven match career with 784 runs at an average of 52.26.

Being away for Test Match duty meant that Walters was a less prolific player for Worcestershire in 1934. However, he still managed three double century opening partnerships with Gibbons, including one of 279 in 190 minutes at Chelmsford, made on the day that Maurice Nichol was found dead in his hotel room.

Walters suffered a breakdown in his health at the end of the 1935 season and he left the game to take up a position with the family business in industry. In 1992 he was chosen as president of the Worcestershire Old Players' Association, a post he held until his death.

Martin Weston
RHB & RM, 1979-93

Born: Worcester, 8 April 1959

Batting career:

M	I	NO	Runs	Av	50
161	258	24	5597	23.91	28
204	*176*	*25*	*3390*	*22.45*	*15*

100	Ct/St
3	76
1	*49*

Bowling career:

O	M	R	W	Av	5wl	10wM
1102.1	268	3204	82	39.07	-	-
869.1	*47*	*3525*	*102*	*34.55*	*-*	*-*

Career best performances:

145* v. Northamptonshire, Northampton, 1984
109 v. Somerset, Taunton, 1982
4-24 v. Warwickshire, Edgbaston, 1988
4-11 v. Hampshire, Worcester, 1988

Martin Weston made his debut for Worcestershire in 1979, playing against Sri Lanka at New Road on the same day as Tim Curtis' first appearance for the side. He was run out for 43 and scored 16 in the second innings, his only appearance before spending the rest of the season in the Second XI, for whom he scored 935 runs in the Second XI Championship. His appearances in the First XI were few until 1982, when he scored his first Championship fifty with 51 at New Road against Gloucestershire, where he shared an opening partnership of 119 with Alan Ormrod. Later that season, when the Pakistani touring side came to New Road, Weston impressed with an aggressive 93, 86 of which were made in a first wicket partnership of 94, with a six and 14 fours from 73 balls. His maiden century followed in 1983, when he scored 115 at Hove, adding 171 with Dipak Patel, Worcestershire's best partnership for the third wicket against Sussex. A career best was achieved in 1984 when he hit 145 not out at New Road against Northamptonshire with 19 fours in 229 minutes. The winning run was scored with two balls to spare, Worcestershire having scored 304 for 6 off 62.4 overs with Weston batting throughout the second innings. At the end of the season he had scored 1,061 runs, his season's best.

Weston was a valued member of the Worcestershire one-day side; in fact, he is the only Worcester-born batsman to score a century in the Sunday League. At Taunton in 1982 he scored 109 off 91 balls, with 5 sixes and 7 fours, but finished on the losing side by two runs. He was a regular member of the sides that won the league in 1987 and 1988, in the latter season sharing the new ball and taking eleven wickets at a miserly 3.16 runs per over with a match winning performance of 4 for 11 off eight overs against Hampshire at New Road.

In the Benson & Hedges semi-final at Trent Bridge in 1990, Weston and Curtis were faced with a Nottinghamshire total of 230 for 6 when they went out to open the innings. They had added 141 by the 35th over before Curtis was bowled, and Graeme Hick then hit 57 off 65 balls. Worcestershire booked their place in their sixth Lord's final with a nine wickets win, with ten balls to spare, and Weston was stranded on 99 not out, a performance that won him the man of the match gold award.

Weston shared a joint benefit with Damian D'Oliveira in 1993 and left the staff at the end of the season. Between 1994 and 1996 he played Minor Counties cricket for Herefordshire.

Fred Wheldon
RHB & WK, 1899-1906

Born: Langley Green, Worcestershire,
1 November 1869
Died: Worcester, 13 January 1924

Batting career:

M	I	NO	Runs	Av	50
138	244	25	4938	22.54	28

100	Ct/St
3	95/1

Bowling career:

O	M	R	W	Av	5wI	10wM
18	2	77	0	-	-	-

Career best performances:

112 v. Somerset, Worcester, 1903

Fred Wheldon made his debut for Worcestershire before they had attained first-class status, first appearing in 1893 and on many occasions in their successful minor counties years between 1895 and 1898. He was already an accomplished soccer player, having made 109 appearances for Small Heath between 1890 and 1896 before joining Aston Villa for their FA Cup and First Division double success in 1896/97. He scored 18 goals in the League and Villa's second in their 3-2 win in the Cup Final over Everton at Crystal Palace. At Nottingham in February 1897 he won the first of his four England caps and scored a hat-trick against Ireland on his debut. From Villa he moved to West Bromwich Albion, Queens Park Rangers, Portsmouth, Worcester City and finally retired from his double career after one season with Coventry City in 1907.

When Worcestershire made their debut in the County Championship at New Road against Yorkshire, Wheldon top scored with 49 not out and at the end of the season had scored 541 runs at an average of 33.81. The following season he hit his maiden century with 100 at Dean Park, Bournemouth and shared a partnership of 186 with William Lowe, which is still Worcestershire's best score for the sixth wicket

against Hampshire.

At New Road in 1903 Wheldon kept wicket for Worcestershire for them for the first time. During Yorkshire's first innings he took his one and only stumping when he dismissed Walker Wainwright off Albert Bird. This was also Wheldon's best season with the bat, scoring 969 runs including the second of his centuries, a career best 112 against Somerset at New Road. This was one of three Worcestershire centuries in a total of 590, with Harry Foster scoring 216 and Fred Bowley 148.

1904 was another successful season – he scored 913 runs and hit the last of his centuries, 103 against Leicestershire at Aylestone Road. He also had his most productive season behind the stumps, keeping wicket on seven occasions and taking 22 catches, including six catches in consecutive matches, against Hampshire at Southampton and Oxford University at Oxford.

During the 1910 season he appeared for Carmarthenshire in the South and West Division of the Minor Counties Championship. A unique family double occurred when his grandson, John Spilsbury, made his one and only appearance for Worcestershire against the Combined Services in 1952. Spilsbury also played soccer for Worcester City, but his grandfather had died nine years before Spilsbury was born.

Norman Whiting
RHB & OB, 1947-52

Born: Wollaston, Stourbridge, 2 October 1920

Batting career:

M	I	NO	Runs	Av	50
59	96	11	1583	18.62	4

100	Ct/St
2	32

Bowling career:

O	M	R	W	Av	5wI	10wM
189	41	657	13	50.53	-	-

Career best performances:

118 v. Essex, Worcester, 1950

2-27 v. Yorkshire, Scarborough, 1951

Norman Whiting first appeared on the scene along with Don Kenyon before the Second World War, playing for Stourbridge in the Birmingham League. He didn't make his first-class debut until 1947, when he opened the innings, in place of Eddie Cooper, with Kenyon against Northamptonshire at Wellingborough School. The leg-breaks of West Indian doctor 'Bertie' Clarke, with match figures of 9 for 100, began a bad run for Worcestershire, with an eight-wicket defeat. They were to lose four of their last five matches heavily, with the other one drawn. Whiting made few appearances until the 1950 season when, at Romford in 'Sonny' Avery's benefit match, Whiting scored 118, hitting 19 fours and adding 198 for the fourth wicket with 'Laddie' Outschoorn in just under three and a half hours. He kept his place for the following dozen matches, hitting 58 at Trent Bridge in another useful partnership of 122 with Outschoorn, but this one for the fifth wicket; at the end of the season, he had scored 620 runs at an average of 20.00.

When Worcestershire declared on 354 for 6 at Hove in 1951, Whiting had scored 68 not out and had shared an unbroken partnership of 119 – a Worcestershire record against Sussex until beaten by Phil Neale and David Humphries at the same venue in 1980.

Whiting missed most of July, but came back in to the side at Scarborough in mid-August in a match that Yorkshire needed to win to have any chance of overtaking Warwickshire in the race for the County Championship. Ronnie Bird declined the opportunity of asking Yorkshire to follow-on after they were dismissed 157 behind, with Whiting taking the wickets of Vic Wilson and Ted Lester for career best figures of 2 for 27. Worcestershire were all out for 92 in their second innings but Dick Howorth, with 6 for 63, bowled them to an eight runs victory.

Whiting scored his second century in the Parks with 111 against Oxford University, followed by 83 in the second innings; but after twelve appearances and 444 runs in 1952 he left the county at the end of the season. He went back to Stourbridge, captaining the side, and joined the Worcestershire Committee as the Stourbridge delegate in 1971, returning to New Road to lead the Second XI in 1974. When Worcestershire joined the Birmingham League in 1975, Whiting was captain until they withdrew at the end of the 1976 season and he has been a member of the general committee since 1976.

Gordon Wilcock

RHB & WK, 1971-78

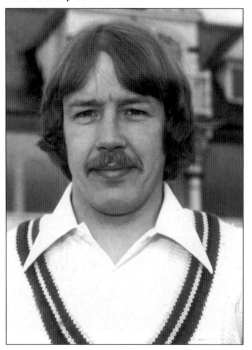

Born: New Malden, Surrey, 26 February 1950

Batting career:

M	I	NO	Runs	Av	50
99	137	31	1697	16.00	1
83	*53*	*17*	*462*	*12.83*	*-*

100	Ct/St
-	177/17
-	*55/9*

Bowling career:

O	M	R	W	Av	5wI	10wM
2	1	3	0	-	-	-

Career best performances:

74 v. Yorkshire, Worcester, 1977

49* v. Warwickshire, Worcester, 1975

Gordon Wilcock was recruited by Worcestershire from Ilkley, the Airedale-Wharfedale League club in Yorkshire, in 1968. He made one Second XI appearance at New Road against Derbyshire and played a full season in 1969. At that time, however, Brian Krikken, father of Derbyshire's Karl, was Second XI wicketkeeper and Wilcock didn't get a chance behind the stumps until the last two matches of the season. In the last match he stumped Northamptonshire's Sarfraz Nawaz and Tony Durose, both off Kevin Griffith at Horton. During this period he was playing for Dudley in the Birmingham League and he played a full Second XI season in 1970, getting his chance in the First XI in 1971.

He made his first-class debut in the Parks in a rain-affected match against Oxford University and kept his place for his Championship debut at New Road against Lancashire in the next game, when he completed his first stumping, Farokh Engineer off Norman Gifford. Regular wicketkeeper Rodney Cass was replaced by Wilcock for the rest of the season and he finished with 36 catches and 4 stumpings. He also performed

well in the Sunday League, and when Ron Headley took over the captaincy following Gifford's injury, he found himself an important member of the side that won that competition. In the match against Hampshire at New Road, Wilcock struck Bob Cottam into the pavilion for six and hit the winning runs, a four off Trevor Jesty, off the fifth ball of the last over.

Wilcock began 1972 well but lost his place to Cass for the last three games, who was to keep him out of the side all through 1973. In the Second XI match at New Road against Glamorgan in 1973 he hit 92 not out and shared an opening stand of 195 with David Stewart.

During the 1974 Championship-winning season, Cass and Wilcock shared the wicketkeeping duties, with 8 and 14 games respectively. At Portsmouth he took six catches in Hampshire's only innings, equalling the Worcestershire Championship record. In all first-class matches he took 41 dismissals to Cass's 23, but it was back into the Second XI after the match at Lord's in July 1975.

Cass was released at the end of the season and Wilcock had a full season in 1976, but his fortune changed once again when David Humphries arrived from Leicestershire. Wilcock left after just one appearance in 1977 against Oxford University.

Born: Amersham, Buckinghamshire, 5 April 1877					

Born: Amersham, Buckinghamshire, 5 April 1877
Died: Abbotts Langley, Herts, 3 March 1962
Batting career:

M	I	NO	Runs	Av	50
154	229	37	2202	11.46	5
100	**Ct/St**				
-	56				

Bowling career:

O	M	R	W	Av	5wl	10wM
5512.5	1053	17127	719	23.82	58	18

Career best performances:

78 v. London County, Worcester, 1900
9-75 v. Oxford University, Oxford, 1904

George Wilson played for Worcestershire in their 1897 and 1898 Minor Counties Championship-winning sides, having been Kidderminster's professional between 1896 and 1898. He made an explosive first-class debut in the first match at New Road against Yorkshire in 1899, where he bowled unchanged in the first innings and took 8 for 70, the best figures for a County Championship debut. At the end of this season he had taken 86 wickets at an average of 21.53, but in August 1900 at New Road he bowled the Derbyshire captain, Samuel Wood, to become the first Worcestershire bowler to take 100 wickets in a season. That same season he hit his career best 78 against W.G. Grace's London County and 97 for the last wicket with Albert Bird. In the same match he dismissed William Quaife (lbw), Foster Robinson (b) and Len Braund (b) off successive deliveries to complete Worcestershire's first hat-trick, and finished with 7 for 71 in their first innings.

The following season Wilson took the first Worcestershire Championship hat-trick at New Road when he dismissed Surrey's Livingstone Walker, Edward Dowson and Fred Stedman with successive balls. For the second consecutive season he took 119 wickets, but this time had 14 five wickets in an innings performances. Whilst Wilson was travelling to Leicester on 27 July 1902, his wife, in Kidderminster, gave birth to a

son, George – he made the first of his 70 appearances for Worcestershire nearly twenty-two years later.

At Cheltenham in 1903 he finished the Gloucestershire first innings with four wickets in five balls and in the second innings finished with a spell of five wickets for six runs. In two consecutive matches against Gloucestershire he had figures of 7 for 51, 5 for 33, 6 for 31 and 7 for 85. Wilson had his career best figures in 1904 at Oxford when he took 9 for 75 in the University's first innings, followed by another two in the second, one of his 18 ten wickets in a match performances, a Worcestershire record until it was beaten by Fred Root in 1925.

When the Australians paid their second visit to New Road in 1905, Wilson took five of their last seven wickets for 31 runs, including his third, and final, hat-trick. A week later at Taunton he had his best match figures of 15 for 142, with 8 for 30 in the first innings and 7 for 112 in the second. Wilson's knack of getting the ball to swerve and lift awkwardly helped Worcestershire to a two day, six wickets win.

Wilson left at the end of 1906 and later appeared for Buckinghamshire (1907-08) and Staffordshire (1912-14).

Bob Wyatt

RHB & RMF, 1946-51

Born: Milford, Surrey, 2 May 1901					
Died: Helford, near Helston, Cornwall, 20 April 1995					
Batting career:					
M	I	NO	Runs	Av	50
86	138	13	4233	33.86	19
100	Ct/St				
6	54				

Bowling career:						
O	M	R	W	Av	5wl	10wM
894.1	282	2387	62	38.50	1	-

Career best performances:

166* v. Sussex, Worcester, 1947

5-43 v. Essex, Worcester, 1948

Bob Wyatt joined Worcestershire in 1946 after a long and successful career with Warwickshire that had begun in 1923. He was appointed captain in 1930, but a disagreement with the committee during the 1937 season resulted in Peter Cranmer being appointed captain for 1938 and when the Second World War came to an end Wyatt joined Worcestershire. Warwickshire agreed to his move and his registration came through in June 1946. By a strange coincidence, the first opportunity he had to appear for Worcestershire was against Warwickshire at Dudley under the captaincy of 'Sandy' Singleton. He struck a rich vein of form in July that season, with 154* against Sussex at New Road, hitting 23 fours, and two weeks later hit 150* at the same venue against Gloucestershire. He finished the season with 914 runs at an average of 41.54.

The following season, when Sussex were again the visitors to New Road, Wyatt recorded his Worcestershire career best of 166 not out, sharing a partnership of 174 with Dick Howorth. This is the record for Worcestershire's fourth wicket against Sussex and an unbroken one of 144 for the sixth wicket with Roly Jenkins. Wyatt was Don Kenyon's partner against Warwickshire, when Kenyon scored his first Championship century. They added 183 for the third wicket at Dudley in three hours to help steer Worcestershire to a seven wickets win with fifteen minutes to spare.

Wyatt was appointed joint captain with Alan White for 1949. By then, however, he was also an England selector, so these duties and his business meant fewer appearances. Together the two captains helped Worcestershire to finish in a respectable third place in the Championship, their best position since 1907.

White retired at the end of that season and Wyatt took over the captaincy for his final two seasons, leading them to sixth place in 1950 and fourth in 1951. At Taunton in 1951 Worcestershire were left to score 214 in under two hours and Wyatt came in when six wickets were down. When Bertie Buse ran in to bowl the last ball of the match, Worcestershire required six to win. Wyatt drove the ball hard and high into the old pavilion for a memorable three wickets win. One week later Somerset arrived for the return match and for Wyatt's final appearance. In his final innings for Worcestershire he scored 59 and shared a third wicket partnership of 103 with Bob Broadbent.

Wyatt scored 39,405 runs in total, 1,839 of which were made in his 40 Test appearances. Some of the Warwickshire wounds were healed when, shortly after his death, the R.E.S. Wyatt stand was opened at Edgbaston.

Hugo Yarnold

RHB & WK, 1938-55

Born: Worcester, 8 July 1917
Died: Leamington Spa, Warwickshire,
13 April 1974

Batting career:

M	I	NO	Runs	Av	50
283	409	68	3620	10.61	6

100	Ct/St
-	459/226

Career best performances:

64 v. Sussex, Hove, 1946

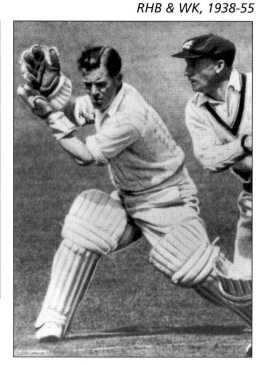

Hugo Yarnold, pictured here with the late Don Bradman, made his Worcestershire debut deputising for Syd Buller behind the stumps at Trent Bridge in Worcestershire's last away match of the 1938 season. Buller was injured in the same road accident in which Charlie Bull was tragically killed on Whit-Sunday evening in 1939 and Yarnold covered for the next nine matches until he was fit again. Yarnold returned after the Second World War and after one season Buller retired, leaving the way open for his long time understudy. At Hove in 1946 Yarnold was chosen for his batting, but kept wicket in the Sussex second innings when Buller was taken ill, scoring 64 during a seventh wicket partnership of 118 with Ronnie Bird.

At the end of his first full season he had held 48 catches and taken an impressive 38 stumpings. This high percentage of stumpings was repeated in 1949 with 44 against 60 catches and was without doubt due mainly to the superb understanding he had with Roly Jenkins' leg-breaks and googlies. This was the first season that a Worcestershire wicketkeeper had taken 100 dismissals in a season, and Roy Booth is the only one to do it since, in 1961 and 1964. At Worcester, Yarnold took nine dismissals in the match against Hampshire, a stumping and three catches in the first innings and three of each in the second, which was a Worcestershire record

until it was equalled by Steve Rhodes against Sussex at Kidderminster in 1988. He also had his best season with the bat, scoring 485 runs at an average of 14.69 and hitting three half-centuries including 56 not out in a last wicket partnership of 92 with Peter Jackson against Warwickshire at New Road.

During the Yorkshire second innings at New Road in 1950 he stumped Gerry Smithson off Dick Howorth for his 320th dismissal, a new Worcestershire record, beating the 319 taken by Ernie Bale between 1908 and 1920. Yarnold's record of 685 lasted until 1964, when it was overtaken by Roy Booth.

Yarnold entered the wicketkeeping record books in 1951 when he took a world record six stumpings and one catch in the Scotland second innings at Broughty Ferry and his seven dismissals is still a Worcestershire record.

Yarnold retired at the end of the 1955 season and became mine host at the Royal George Inn in Tunnel Hill. He joined the first-class umpires list in 1957, standing in three Test matches. On his way home from umpiring Northamptonshire v. Essex at Wellingborough School, he was killed at Leamington Spa in a road accident.

Younis Ahmed

LHB & LM, 1979-83

Born: Jullundur, India, 20 October 1947

Batting career:

M	I	NO	Runs	Av	50
85	133	30	5486	53.26	30
81	*79*	*8*	*2411*	*33.95*	*12*

100	Ct/St
13	45
4	*10*

Bowling career:

O	M	R	W	Av	5wI	10wM
178.5	33	521	12	43.41	-	-
203.5	*3*	*912*	*26*	*35.07*	-	-

Career best performances:

221* v. Nottinghamshire, Trent Bridge, 1979

115 v. Yorkshire, Worcester, 1980*

3-33 v. Oxford University, Oxford, 1979

4-37 v. Northamptonshire, Northampton, 1980

Younis Ahmed was released by Surrey at the end of the 1978 season, having spent fourteen turbulent seasons at The Oval after making his first-class debut as a fourteen year-old in Pakistan for the Inter Board Schools XI in March 1962. Younis made four Test appearances for Pakistan, twice in 1969/70, and returned 17 years and 111 days later to play two more. The first Worcestershire match of the 1979 season had a delayed start because the roller handle had been crushed in to the pitch and repairs were required. Rain and sleet also interrupted Younis' debut against Somerset, but when he got in he scored 52. Worcestershire won their first match of the season in mid-June when they beat Lancashire at New Road by six wickets, thanks to an unbroken partnership of 144 between Younis and Ted Hemsley in 28 overs, 100 of the runs coming after tea in forty-six minutes. A little later in the season he shared another big partnership, this time with Alan Ormrod, 281 at Trent Bridge, a Worcestershire record for the fourth wicket. Younis hit a career best 221 not out and at the end of the season he had an aggregate of 1,539 runs at an average of 69.95, and lay second to Geoff Boycott in the national averages.

That season he hit two centuries in the Sunday League and became the first left-hander to reach an aggregate of 4,000 runs in the competition. In 1980 he reached his 1,000 league runs for Worcestershire in just 24 innings, then only the third batsman, following Roy Virgin and Roger Knight, to aggregate 1,000 runs for two different counties.

The 1980 season was not quite so successful for Younis, although he did hit two centuries, including 109, the first one ever at Cleethorpes where Nottinghamshire were staging their first Championship match. Early in 1980 he scored 115 in the Benson & Hedges Cup match against Yorkshire at New Road, for which he won his only man of the match award for Worcestershire.

Three centuries in 1982 helped him towards 1,637 runs in 1981, and he had four the following season when he scored 1,247 runs, the prelude to his troublesome season in 1983. After two not out innings of 10 and 32 in the first two Championship matches, Younis placed a bet on Leicestershire to beat Worcestershire in a Sunday League match. The match was abandoned because of the weather, but the committee found that this conduct was unacceptable and Younis was asked to leave the club. He moved on to Glamorgan where he played out his career until 1986.